COMPARISON OF DIFFERENT TECHNIQUES TO MEASURE ADIPOSITY IN CHILDREN

SAKSHI KAPOOR BHUSHAN

CONTENTS

CHAPTER 1.0: INTRODUCTION   1

CHAPTER 2.0: REVIEW OF LITERATURE   4

2.1   The global problem of childhood obesity   5

2.2   Childhood obesity in the developing countries   7

2.3   Childhood obesity in India   8

2.4   Defining childhood obesity   10

2.5   Methods of measuring body fatness   14

     2.5.1   Models and concepts in body composition   14
     2.5.2   Laboratory methods of body composition   17
     2.5.3   Field methods of body composition   20

2.6   Methods of measuring distribution of body fat   31

2.7   Obesity based on body fat as a criterion   34

2.8   Factors leading to childhood obesity   35

CHAPTER 3.0: METHODOLOGY

3.1   Selection of subjects   41

3.2	Locale	43
3.3	Sampling technique and sample size	44
3.4	Period of data collection	45
3.5	Age profile	45
3.6	Tools and techniques for data collection	45
	3.6.1 General information	46
	3.6.2 Anthropometric measurements	47
	3.6.3 Techniques to measure adiposity in children in field	53
	3.6.4 Physical activity pattern and food habits	59
3.7	Selection of government school boys	61
3.8	Quality control	62
	3.8.1 Quality control methods for equipments	62
	3.8.2 Quality control methods for anthropometric measurements	62
3.9	Statistical analysis	63

CHAPTER 4.0: RESULTS

4.1	General profile of the study population	66
	4.1.1 Type of family	67
	4.1.2 Number of children in the family	67
	4.1.3 Education status of the parents	68
	4.1.4 Occupation of the parents	69
4.2	Anthropometric profile of the study population	70
	4.2.1 Weight	70
	4.2.2 Height	85
	4.2.3 BMI	99
	4.2.4 Circumferences	111
	4.2.5 Fatfolds	117
4.3	Body fat estimation	123
	4.3.1 Techniques for body fat estimation	124
	4.3.2 Fat Mass Index	136
	4.3.3 Percent body fat (%BF)	138
	4.3.4 Distribution of body fat	142
	4.3.5 Relationship between BMI and %BF	146

4.4	Physical activity pattern and food habits		160
	4.4.1	Physical activity	160
	4.4.2	Food habits	166
4.5	Public school vs government school boys (9yr old)		175
	4.5.1 Prevalence of under-nutrition and over-nutrition (WHO 2007)		175
	4.5.2 Prevalence of adiposity		177

CHAPTER 5.0: SUMMARY AND CONCLUSIONS   179

1.0 INTRODUCTION

The prevalence of childhood overweight and obesity is increasing worldwide (Monteiro et al, 1995; Flegal et al, 2001; Wang and Dietz, 2002). Available data from studies in India also indicate that the prevalence of over-nutrition is rising in school children especially in those from urban high-income group (Ramachandran et al, 2002; Vijaylakshmi et al, 2002). Studies carried out by the Nutrition Foundation of India in the nineties in Public schools in Delhi showed that over-nutrition begins right from play school age (4-5 years) (Sharma et al, 2006). Low levels of physical activity, diets rich in fats and oils, sugars and less fiber are some important factors resulting in over-nutrition (Popkin et al, 2002; Kapoor et al, 2003).

Currently, body mass index (BMI) is the most commonly used index for assessing over-nutrition both in adults and in children. BMI is easy to measure in clinical and epidemiological studies but it does not directly measure body fat. Prevalence of obesity in a population is determined as the proportion above a BMI cutoff-point. This is thought to represent number of individuals with excess amount of body fat (Bhat et al, 2005).

The relationship between BMI and total body fat differs in different populations. Since BMI does not distinguish between weight associated with muscle mass from weight due to excess body fat (adiposity), hence a given BMI does not correspond to the same degree of fatness in different population groups. Also, it does not provide any information on the location of adiposity (Dietz et al, 1999; Bedogni et al, 2003). Available data in adults indicate that Indians have a higher body fat and higher abdominal adiposity for a given BMI as compared to Caucasians and African Americans (Deurenberg et al, 1998; Chandalia et al, 1999; Yajnik et al, 2003; Arora and Siddhu, 2005). Norgan (1990) showed that rural individuals from India, Ethiopia and Papua New Guinea had 12, 7, 1 percent body fat respectively, for a BMI of 20 kg/m^2. McKeigue and colleagues (1991) found that migrants from India, Pakistan and Bangladesh who settled in England had very high rates of coronary heart disease (CHD) than the general population, even though they had lower BMI. In another study, in Indians, central obesity was found to have a more important association with hyperglycemia than generalized obesity (Shelgikar et al, 1991). Since adiposity i.e. excessive fat deposition and deposition in specific areas i.e. abdominal fat appears to be the major risk factor responsible for development of insulin resistance, diabetes and cardiovascular disease in adults (McKeigue, 1997), it is essential that efforts be made to assess body composition of Indians in terms of fat mass and its distribution.

Studies have also reported that obesity and increased fat deposition begin in early childhood (Rolland-Cachera et al, 1987; Eriksson et al, 2003; Kaur et al, 2005). Although the long-term effects of overweight and obesity on morbidity and mortality in children have not yet been well documented, several studies suggest that obesity in childhood is followed by serious consequences in adulthood and thus increases the risk of non-communicable diseases and premature death in adulthood (Guo et al, 1994; Guillaume, 1999; Raitakari et al, 2005). Given the increase in the prevalence of childhood obesity in India, accurate methods for determining body composition in children is of utmost importance.

The easiest technique to use in field situations is the model in which human body is divided into two compartments (2-C model): fat mass (FM) and fat free mass (FFM) (Bhat et al, 2005). Two such techniques are anthropometry (using multiple fatfold thickness) and bioelectrical impedance analysis (BIA), which indirectly measure body density and body water respectively.

Fatfold measurements using calipers, are taken at sites where fat is most abundant subcutaneously namely peripheral fat (biceps and triceps) and truncal fat (subscapular and suprailiac) (Jelliffe et al, 1989). The sum of these fatfolds is used in age and gender specific regression equations, of which there are many available, for the prediction of body composition (Kurpad, 2003). A newer technique of body fat assessment is the BIA measurement; the equipment is portable, technique is non-invasive and is a rapid method for body composition analysis with significantly fewer technical problems as compared to the fatfold technique (NIH, 1996). In healthy subjects, several studies showed that this method offers valid and reproducible results when population-specific regression equations are used. However, it is not clear whether these field techniques offer completely comparable results for assessing body fat.

The objective of the present study was to compare different techniques for assessment of body fat and its distribution in 6-14 year old children studying in public schools.

Specific objectives

- To anthropometrically assess boys and girls in the 6-14 year age group studying in public schools

- To assess adiposity (body fat) in these children using two techniques: anthropometry (using multiple fatfolds) and BIA

- To assess distribution of body fat in these children

- To derive the relationship between BMI and adiposity in these children

- To study the physical activity pattern and food habits in a small sub sample of these children with high and low BMI

- To assess the magnitude of differences in anthropometry and body fat as compared to government school boys

2.0 REVIEW OF LITERATURE

Our early ancestors were hunter-gatherers confronted with the constant challenge to find enough food to survive. Dependent on a diet predominantly derived from plants, but only occasionally from animal sources, the capacity to store energy to defend against seasonal food shortages and famine was an essential survival mechanism. It seems that the primordial imperative to consume food when available and store energy in the expectation of shortages remains one of the most powerful biological factors that increase our vulnerability in times of enduring plenty (IOTF, 2006) (Figure 2.1).

Although several genes have been identified as having a role in obesity, what is not yet fully understood is the complex interaction between genes and environment, the endocrine system and diet, and the way the brain's subtle command pathways that control energy balance may be easily overridden to allow the primitive drive to store food to dominate.

Figure 2.1: The Shape of things to come - cover of The Economist, December 13-19, 2003

The human race is facing a novel and enormous health challenge due to the rapidly unfolding global epidemic of obesity. The prevalence of obesity in all age groups poses such a serious problem that the World Health Organization (WHO) has described it as a 'global epidemic'. Unprecedented changes in the nature of our diet and the way of living in recent years, are now contributing not only to almost ubiquitous weight gain, but to a dramatic growth in related chronic diseases. The transformation of agricultural production, the restructuring of the food supply and its distribution mechanisms, as well as urbanization and the development of predominantly sedentary modes of work and leisure, are generating a quantum shift in the scale of nutrition and activity related chronic diseases, now affecting billions of people in both the developed and developing countries.

These changes have already accelerated the rise in mean body weights of most adult populations, with an exceptional impact upon children. The increased burden of childhood obesity in the last few years involves not only its increase in prevalence, but also its development at earlier ages and the more frequent occurrence of its associated co-morbidities, such as diabetes mellitus type 2, cardiovascular diseases, and hypertension (Freedman et al, 1999).

2.1 THE GLOBAL PROBLEM OF CHILDHOOD OBESITY

Childhood obesity is one of the most serious public health challenges of the 21st century. The problem is global and is steadily affecting many low-income and middle-income countries, particularly in urban settings.

In 2004, the WHO estimated that approximately 22 million children under the age of five years were overweight or obese. According to a report from the International Obesity Task Force (IOTF, 2006), at least 155 million children aged 5-17 years are overweight, including up to 45 million classified as obese, accounting for 2-3% of the worlds children aged 5-17 years. The calculated global prevalence of overweight (including obesity) in children aged 5-17 years is 10%, and the prevalence varies from over 30% in America to <2% in sub

Saharan Africa. In the United Kingdom (UK), there are approximately one million obese individuals who are less than 16 years of age and the situation is getting worse (WHO, 2007). In Europe, the prevalence of obesity has tripled in the last two decades – a particularly alarming trend. If no action is taken and obesity continues to increase at the same rate as in the 1990s, an estimated 15 million children and adolescents in Europe will be obese by 2010 (WHO, 2007).

The number of school-age children affected will almost double by 2010 compared with the most recent surveys conducted up to year 2003 (Duncan et al, 2004) (Table 2.1). Assuming the trends observed in 2006 continue on a linear basis, they would give a projection of approximately 41% of children in the eastern Mediterranean region and 38% of children in Europe as a whole being overweight. In both North and South America, obesity prevalence in children is forecast to rise to 15.2%. In the Pacific region the figure may rise to 7%, while in Asia – where the smaller numbers classified with obesity understate the severity of the problem, a threefold increase to 5.3% is expected (Wang and Lobstein, 2006).

Table 2.1: Overweight and obesity in school aged children by global region						
WHO Regions (most recent surveys)	Recent surveys		Projected 2006		Projected 2010	
	Overweight (including obesity) %	Obesity %	Overweight (including obesity) %	Obesity %	Overweight (including obesity) %	Obesity %
Africa (1987-2003)	1.6	0.2	-	-	-	-
Americas (1988-2002)	27.7	9.6	40	13.2	46.4	15.2
Eastern Med (1992-2001)	23.5	5.9	35.3	9.4	41.7	11.5
Europe (1992-2003)	25.5	5.4	31.8	7.9	38.2	10.0
South East Asia (1997-2002)	0.6	1.5	16.6	3.3	22.9	5.3
West Pacific (1993-2000)	12.0	2.3	20.8	5.0	27.2	7.0
Source: Wang and Lobstein, 2006						

2.2 CHILDHOOD OBESITY IN THE DEVELOPING COUNTRIES

The problem of obesity, until recently considered only a problem of the affluent nations, is now a remarkable amplifier of diabetes, high blood pressure and high cholesterol levels, the very basis for the biggest health problem of cardiovascular disease, in low and middle income countries. Since both under-nutrition and over-nutrition are seen simultaneously in developing countries, the double burden of diseases makes the situation more difficult. Since 1986, several surveys in preschool children show increasing obesity in most countries in Latin America and the Caribbean, along with the Middle East and North Africa, which is comparable with prevalence rates of childhood obesity seen in the United States of America (USA) (Martorell et al, 2000). Recent studies have suggested that at present around 2 million US adolescents – one third of all overweight youngsters – are affected by the metabolic syndrome (a cluster of risks for heart disease and an early death), compared with just under 1 million estimated less than a decade earlier (Duncan et al, 2004). The problem is not confined to the USA or to developed countries, but affects more than one in five children in many countries, and is increasing rapidly in others (IOTF, 2006) (Figure 2.2).

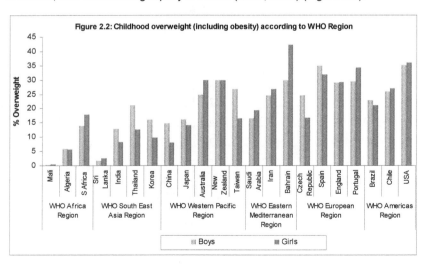

Data from the China's National Nutrition and Health Survey, 2002, suggest that 21 million Chinese children are overweight or obese and that the prevalence of overweight and obesity in children aged 7-18 years increased 28 times and obesity increased four times between 1985 and 2000, a trend that was particularly marked in boys (Wu, 2006). The prevalence of obesity in 5 to 12 year old children in Thailand increased from 12.2% to 15.6% over a period of 2 years and from 16.0% to 24.0% between years 2002 to 2007 in New Delhi, India (Misra and Khurana, 2008).

2.3 CHILDHOOD OBESITY IN INDIA

Recent trends in Indian population indicate a rise in obesity both in adults as well as children in direct correlation with better socioeconomic status and urban habitation (Misra and Khurana, 2008).

Table 2.2 summarizes studies reporting the prevalence of overweight and obesity in children and adolescents from different parts of the country. The prevalence rates vary depending on diverse criteria used. However all studies show a high prevalence of overweight and obesity among children and adolescents in urban India.

The results of studies among children and adolescents (4 -18 years) from parts of Delhi, Maharashtra and South India reveal a high prevalence of overweight and obesity (9.9% to 29.0%). A study in Delhi on affluent school children showed the prevalence of obesity to be 8.3% and 5.5% in boys and girls respectively (Kapil et al, 2002). Similar results were reported by another study among 4-18 years in a Delhi private school (Sharma et al, 2006). In Pune, Maharashtra, studies done on 1228 boys in the age group of 10-15 years showed that the prevalence of obesity to be 5.7% whereas the prevalence of overweight was 19.9%.

Table 2.2: Childhood obesity in India

Place	Author	Year	Age (yr)	Sample size (n)	Criteria for measuring overweight/obesity	Overweight (%)		Obese (%)	
						Boys	Girls	Boys	Girls
Delhi	Kapil et al	2002	10-16	563 B 307 G	Overweight/obesity: age- and gender-specific BMI (IOTF)	23.1	27.7	8.3	5.5
Chennai	Subramanyam et al	2003	10-15	610 G	Overweight: BMI ≥ 85th percentile, obesity: BMI ≥ 95th percentile	-	9.7	-	6.2
Pune	Khadilkar et al	2004	10-15	1288 B	WHO BMI cut-offs Overweight: BMI = 25 – 29.9 kg/m^2, obese: BMI ≥ 30 kg/m^2	19.9	-	5.7	-
Amritsar	Sidhu et al	2005	10-15	323 B 317 G	Overweight: BMI ≥ 85th percentile, obesity: BMI ≥ 95th percentile	9.9	12.0	5.0	6.3
Delhi	Sharma et al	2006	4-17	2497 B 1902 G	Overweight/obesity: age- and gender-specific BMI (IOTF)	23.7	20.7	7.0	4.7
Delhi	Kaur et al	2008	5-18	3298 B 3070 G	Overweight/obesity: age- and gender-specific BMI (IOTF)	14.7	16.0	6.5	7.1
Pune	Rao et al	2008	9-16	1146 B 1036 G	Overweight/obesity: age- and gender-specific BMI (IOTF)	24.7	21.3	-	-
Chennai	Ramachandran et al	2002	13-18	4700	Overweight/obesity: age- and gender-specific BMI (IOTF)	Overweight: P = 23.5; G = 4.2			
Delhi	Marwaha et al	2006	5-17	12645 P 8840 G	Overweight/obesity: age- and gender-specific BMI (IOTF)	Overweight: Boys: P = 16.8; G = 2.7 Girls: P = 19.0; G = 2.1			
Delhi	Bhardwaj et al	2008	14-17	2552 P 941 G	Overweight/obesity: age- and gender-specific BMI (IOTF)	Overweight/obesity: P = 29.0; G = 11.3			
Ludhiana	Mohan et al	2004	11-17	2467 U 859 R	WHO BMI cut-offs Overweight: BMI = 25 – 29.9 kg/m^2, obese: BMI ≥ 30 kg/m^2	U= overweight 11.6, obesity 2.4; R= overweight 4.7, obesity 3.6			
Ernakulum (Kerala)	Manuraj et al	2007	5-16	24842	Overweight: BMI ≥ 85th percentile, obesity: BMI ≥ 95th percentile	Overweight: P = 7.2; G = 3.2 U = 8.7; R = 3.8			

B=Boys, G=Girls; P=Private schools; G=Government schools; U=Urban; R=Rural

Furthermore, overweight is more common in urban areas as compared to rural areas. Results of a study from Ludhiana, Punjab, revealed that children in the age group of 11–17 years residing in urban areas were more overweight (11.6%) compared to children from rural areas (4.7%). Similar results have been reported from other parts of the country (Manuraj et al, 2007).

Studies also show that prevalence is higher in privately funded schools as compared to government funded schools (Ramachandran et al, 2002; Marwaha et al, 2006; Bhardwaj et al, 2008).

2.4 DEFINING CHILDHOOD OBESITY

The WHO (2000) defines overweight and obesity as "abnormal or excessive fat accumulation that presents a risk to health". Hence, the diagnosis of obesity should ideally be based on accurate direct or indirect measure of total fat mass. However, measuring the level of adipose tissue and determining when it is likely to affect health is not an easy task, especially in children and adolescents. This is because:

- Body composition changes during childhood and adolescence. The proportion of fat and lean tissue in the body not only varies between boys and girls, but also changes with age and physical maturity making it even more difficult to determine what is physiologically normal either for an individual or for a population (Poskitt and Edmunds, 2008). Figure 2.3 shows how estimated fatness as percent body fat (%BF) varies from birth to 10 years of age in a reference child as described by Fomon et al (1982). Table 2.3 gives the %BF estimates at different ages during childhood and adolescence as given by various investigators.

Physiologically the age related changes in body composition suggest that the body prepares for periods of vigorous growth (early years, puberty and pregnancy) by laying down fat which can then fuel subsequent growth.

Percentage body fat shows dramatic increase in the first year of life and gradually declines until around 5 years of age (Fomon 1974). The values of %BF are low at birth, but increase rapidly until 3-4 months in boys and 6 months in girls and then decrease slowly throughout preschool years and middle childhood, with larger values in girls than boys. From around 5 years onwards to 10 years of age, children begin to increase rates of fat deposition again: the adiposity rebound. Boys and girls both gain body fat early in adolescence. The adolescent growth spurt in girls is smaller, peaks earlier and finishes sooner than in boys (Patton and Viner, 2007). Around puberty girls tend to accumulate more fat than boys and girls with early puberty tend to become obese more readily than late maturing girls.

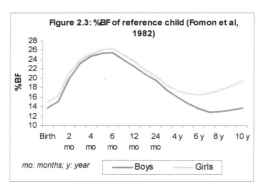

Figure 2.3: %BF of reference child (Fomon et al, 1982)

Slight sex differences in estimated body fat content have been detected in children and even in infants, but it is not until adolescence that the difference becomes striking. Boys who are growing well but have relatively delayed puberty may continue relatively high rates of fat deposition until their pubertal growth spurt. Some of these boys may become overweight or obese, but if wisely managed, this overweight or obesity should disappear with growth spurt and changes in body composition that accompany this (Bogin, 1999). Post puberty, the gain in body fat stops, even reverses temporarily in boys, while girls continue to put on fat as adolescence proceeds. The adult years see a further accumulation in both sexes (Forbes, 1978).

Table 2.3: Estimates of %BF at different ages in childhood

Age	Widdowson[a]	Fomon[b]		Rauh and Schumsky[c]		McCarthy[d]	
	Both sexes	Boys	Girls	Boys	Girls	Boys	Girls
26 wks gestation	1	-	-	-	-	-	-
Term infant	16	14	15	-	-	-	-
4 months	-	25	25	-	-	-	-
12 months	-	23	24	-	-	-	-
5 years	-	-	-	13	15	16	18
10 years	-	-	-	18	20	18	23
15 years	-	-	-	11	23	16	24
18 years	-	-	-	12	25	15	25

[a] *Analysis of chemical composition of body*
[b] *Derived from total body water estimates*
[c] *Derived from fatfold measurements*
[d] *Derived from bioelectrical impedance measurements*

Source: Poskitt and Edmunds, 2008

- Children also undergo chemical maturation between birth and adulthood which presents additional difficulties in the measurement of body composition in children, influencing the theoretical assumptions through which physical measurements are converted into body composition values. For more than a century biologists have known that young tissues differ from old in chemical composition. The young body has a higher proportion of water and a lower proportion of ash; young bones contain less calcium, young muscle less potassium, and the ratio of extracellular fluid volume to intracellular fluid volume declines during growth (Forbes, 1978). Fomon et al (1982) published a paper describing the "reference child", attempting to describe the changes in body composition between birth and 10 years. This dataset has been widely used and presents reference values for the hydration, potassium content and density of FFM, thereby allowing the calculation of body composition values from various body composition methods like hydrometry, potassium counting and densitometry. However this dataset extends only to 10 years.

Since measuring body fat is difficult, health care professionals often rely on other means to diagnose obesity. In large-scale population surveys and clinical/public health screening, anthropometric measures based on weight and height, are the most commonly used methods for defining overweight and obesity in children and adolescents. BMI-for-age i.e. weight for a particular height for a particular age (weight/height^2 for age) has achieved international acceptance as the basic measure for clinical assessment of obesity in children and adolescents and is well correlated with adiposity (Pietrobelli et al, 1998). For children, BMI varies considerably with age, so generally the BMI of a child is compared with the BMI of a reference population of children of the same sex and age. A variety of reference data sets for BMI in childhood exist. The use of reference values embraces the notion of a norm or desirable target and the classification of individuals and populations as normal, overweight, or obese is highly dependent on the reference data used (de Onis, 1996).

In the United States, the Centers for Disease Control and Prevention (CDC) 2000 growth charts for the United States were developed from five nationally representative survey data sets [the National Health Examination Surveys (NHES) II and III in the 1960s, the National Health and Nutrition Examination Survey (NHANES) I and II in the 1970s and NHANES III, 1988–94]. They included, for the first time, sex-specific BMI-for-age growth curves for ages 2 through 19 years by single month of age (Kuczmarski et al, 2002).

Cole et al (2000) published a set of smoothed sex-specific BMI cutoff values for 6-18 year olds based on six nationally representative data sets from Brazil, Great Britain, Hong Kong, the Netherlands, Singapore and the United States. The US data used were the same as those from which the 2000 CDC growth charts were derived, except that no NHANES III data were used. These values, often referred to as the International Obesity Task Force (IOTF) cutoff values, represent cutoff points chosen as the percentiles that matched the adult cutoffs of a BMI of 25 and 30 kg/m^2 at age 18 years. A number of reports have shown that the IOTF-BMI cutoffs substantially underestimate the prevalence of childhood obesity in different populations (Kain et al, 2002; Fu et al, 2003). Wang and Wang (2002) reported that compared to the 1977 NCHS reference, in a sample of 1678 Russian children aged 6–9 y, the IOTF cutoffs yielded a prevalence of obesity of about half that estimated using the NCHS reference (11.1% vs. 20.5%).

In order to facilitate global comparisons of trends in childhood and adolescent obesity rates, the WHO 2007 has recently released BMI-for-age growth charts for 5-19 year olds.

However, body composition in terms of FM inferred from simple anthropometric measurements such as weight and height are often not sufficient to fully explore relations between body fat and alterations in human health. There are a number of other methods available to assess body fat ranging from those that actually measure body components to those that predict them. Some of the techniques are very advanced and can be used in well equipped laboratories. Other techniques are less advanced, less laborious and therefore suitable in field and epidemiological studies.

2.5 METHODS OF MEASURING BODY FATNESS

2.5.1 Models and concepts in body composition

Clinicians and nutritionists are faced with a wide choice of methods for assessing body composition. Most body composition methods are based upon the classic 2-component models of Siri (1961) and Brozek et al (1963) in which the body consists of two chemically distinct compartments (2-C model), FM and FFM. This was the earliest attempt at describing *in vivo* body composition and is still the most common method today.

To achieve a greater precision in 2-C model, the FFM compartment is sub-divided into a water and water free compartment (Kurpad, 2003). Thus if an independent estimate of the total body water (TBW) can be made and if the water content of FFM is regarded as constant and FM is anhydrous, the measurement of TBW can be used to derive FFM and FM. Alternatively, we can regard the body as a 3-component (3-C model) made up of FM, TBW and dry FFM (mainly protein and minerals).

Further precision can be achieved by further dividing the anhydrous FFM into mineral and mineral free compartments. Thus, if we add a third measurement, e.g. of mineral content (M) or of total body protein (TBP), we can view the body as a 4-component model (4-C model), FM, and the constituents of FFM, namely TBW, M and TBP (Norgan, 2005).

All of these *in vivo* measurements rest on certain assumptions. The assumption of a constant composition of FFM is central to the 2-C model and methods. As more components are measured in 3-C and 4-C models and methods, fewer assumptions are required and these are regarded as superior to 2-C methods. However, they are more difficult to perform, in terms of costs and expertise. They are normally used in a clinical setting but have an important role in the study of healthy body composition by validating simpler methods (Norgan, 2005). The methods available for the measurement of body composition are shown in Table 2.4. The majority of these are laboratory methods, or are expensive or require competent technical expertise. The most commonly used are the 2-C techniques of densitometry and hydrometry. The most commonly used field techniques are fatfold thickness and bio-impedance analysis, although the body mass index (BMI) is widely used as a measure of level of fatness. The apparent simplicity, speed and cheapness of some of the field techniques have led to their popularity in an unquestioning way.

Table 2.4: Methods of measurement of body composition

In vitro

Anatomical dissection: muscle, skeleton, adipose tissue, viscera

Chemical analysis: water, fat, protein, mineral, carbohydrate

In vivo

Whole body

    Densitometry

    Hydrometry

    Element analysis; K, Ca, N, C by in vivo neutron activation analysis

    Dual energy X-ray absorptiometry (DEXA)

    Magnetic resonance imaging (MRI)

Regional

    Fatfolds, subcutaneous adipose tissue

    Computed tomography (CT)

    DEXA

    MRI

Areas

    Fatfolds + circumferences

    CT

    DEXA

    MRI

Estimations

    Regional measurements for estimating whole body composition
        Fatfold thickness
        Near infra-red interactance (NIRI)

    Whole body measurements for estimating whole body composition
        BMI
        BIA

Source: Norgan, 2005

2.5.2 Laboratory methods of body composition

Densitometry

Densitometry or underwater weighing has been long considered the laboratory "gold standard" for body composition assessment (Wilmore and Costill, 1999; Lohman and Going, 2006). This technique requires complete underwater immersion after maximal exhalation, multiple trials and measurement of residual lung volume to estimate body density, assuming the body is composed of two distinct components: FM and FFM (Lukaski, 1987).

During underwater weighing, the densities of FM and FFM are assumed and have been derived from animal studies, cadaver analysis and studies of the individual constituents. These assumptions may or may not be true, since the density of the FFM varies with age (Wells et al, 1999). Although these variations are small, they can result in 5-10% errors in the measurement of body fat (Kurpad, 2003). The measurement of body density by underwater weighing is highly repeatable such that the precision is equal to 0.7 kg fat (Coward et al, 1998). In this respect it outperforms many other techniques.

A variety of equations are available to estimate fat from body density, most widely accepted equations are those by Siri (1961) and Brozek (1963). These equations have been applied to various populations including children (Durnin and Rahaman, 1967; Brook, 1971; Johnston et al, 1988; Deurenberg et al, 1990).

Not everyone can perform the manoeuvers necessary for underwater weighing. Also, this approach is time consuming, requires fairly sophisticated instrumentation, is difficult to carry out and is contraindicated or impractical in certain clinical subgroups such as the elderly, hypertensive individuals, subjects who are uncomfortable being immersed in water especially children and those who have limited control on respiration (Wilmore and Costill, 1999). There is now an air displacement plethysmographic apparatus (BOD POD) available which does not require immersion (Norgan, 2005).

Hydrometry

Hydrometry or doubly labeled water technique (DLW) is a suitable and widely used alternative to densitometry. The procedure is non invasive. TBW can be measured by the dilution of an isotopic tracer such as the stable non-radioactive isotope of hydrogen, deuterium (Norgan, 2005). Other isotopes have drawbacks, tritium is radioactive and $H_2\ ^{18}O$ is very expensive. A dose of water labelled with the isotope is given and, following equilibration, enrichment of the body water pool is measured using samples of saliva, urine, or blood (Davies and Wells, 1994). Samples are generally analyzed by isotope ratio mass spectrometry.

The use of stable isotopes (deuterium and oxygen 18) makes this method applicable to children of all ages and the methodological precision is 1-2% (Coward et al, 1988).

Estimation of FFM from TBW is a preferred method as long as the appropriate (age or maturation adjusted) conversion constants are used. The use of body water measurement to estimate FFM assumes constant water content of the FFM among healthy children of various ages. However, in disease states variability in FFM hydration may be substantially higher, owing to either over hydration or under hydration (Lohman and Going, 2006). There is considerable evidence that prepubescent and pubescent children between 6-14 years of age have a higher hydration level than young adults.

Isotope dilution is simple to carry out and requires minimal subject cooperation. It has proved particularly valuable in infants and toddlers because of the low compliance required, and can easily be used in field studies. One drawback of the method as a field technique is the 3-5 hour period necessary for dilution and equilibration of the tracer (Norgan, 2005). It could prove a useful clinical tool for individuals where normal hydration can be assumed. However, this method is costly and very few places in India have the required infrastructure for carrying out this technique. It is mainly used for assessment of energy expenditure in free-living persons. It does not give individual cost of activities. It gives cumulative total energy expenditure over a period of time. Studies using the DLW technique are the basis for energy requirements of children and adolescents (FAO/WHO/UNU, 2004).

DEXA

DEXA is a relatively new whole body and regional body composition technique that is being used increasingly in medicine and biology. It allows the body to be described as a 3-C model of mineral, mineral free soft tissue and FM. This technique uses a whole body scanner and is based on the assumption that amount of photon energy absorbed differs in different components of the body. It is relatively quick, radiation doses are low, less costly and less cumbersome procedure for accurate estimation of body fat (Jebb and Wells, 2005). Whole body DEXA can clearly give information on the bone, FFM, FM and also distribution of FM (Lohman and Going, 2006). Increasingly, DEXA is being used as a "gold standard" for validation of equations for body composition from anthropometric indices and BIA.

Ellis et al (2000) have developed reference models for children and adolescents using DEXA in a population of black, white and Hispanic children from 5-19 years of age. In general, their results confirm older estimates of FFM and FM by Fomon et al (1982) and Haschke (1989) using indirect estimates of body composition from the literature. Sopher et al (2004) compared DEXA with a 4-C model adjusted for mineral and water in a large sample of 411 children and adolescents, 6-18 years of age. Close average (approximately 1%) agreement was found between the two methods; they were highly correlated ($r^2 = 0.85$), and prediction accuracy was good (SEE = 3.7%).

CT and MRI

CT involves X-ray radiation doses at higher levels than DEXA and, as a consequence, does not have the same widespread use. A number of exposures are made and complex reconstructive software is used to generate cross-sectional areas, volumes and masses of tissues.

MRI utilizes the property of elements with unpaired protons or neutrons, such as hydrogen and carbon, to resonate and dissipate energy after exposure to a magnetic field. The energy released is used to build up images of cross-sectional areas. No radiation is produced and so the method can be used for repeated measurements and for children. MRI has been used in children to study physiological conditions such as adiposity (Weiss et al, 2003) and growth and development (Brambilla et al, 1994; Brambilla et al, 1999).The disadvantages of MRI are the expense of the apparatus and measurement and the long scan time, 10-15 minutes, during which time the subject must remain still (Norgan, 2005). However, MRI is being used for calibration of field methods designed to measure body fat and skeletal muscle *in vivo* (Ross et al, 2000).

2.5.3 Field methods of body composition

Body weight

Weight, though a crude measure of the body's energy reserves, yet is without doubt the most common method by which obesity is documented. Earlier, under-nutrition was the major problem among children; weight-for-age was the most widely used indicator for assessment of under-nutrition in community settings. In clinical settings, weight-for-age and height-for-age were used as the two indices for assessment of under-nutrition. However, weight-for-age alone is inappropriate as an indicator as it may misclassify short children who are overweight for their height as undernourished or normal. Similarly, tall and lean children will be misclassified as normal using weight-for-age even though they are actually undernourished. In view of this, weight for a particular height for a particular age (weight/height^2 for age) or BMI-for-age has been adopted as the basic measure for clinical assessment of obesity in children and adolescents (Maynard et al, 2001). However, a recent global survey on child growth monitoring practices (de Onis et al, 2004) showed that weight-for-age was the anthropometric indicator universally used (97% of countries), while only 23% of the countries used weight-for-height, with BMI being rarely used.

BMI

Currently BMI is the most widely used index as a surrogate of body fat content. It has been shown to be a good indicator of adiposity in adults (Pietrobelli et al, 1998) and there is a wide body of evidence which links increasing BMI to increased risk of morbidity and mortality in adults (Freedman et al, 1999). Although the relationship between BMI and adiposity is not as strong in children as it is in adults it still appears to be a useful tool for identifying overweight and obese children (Wells and Fewtrell, 2006). Although BMI can be used as a measure of under- and over-nutrition, its relation with body composition per se is controversial in children and adolescents.

BMI is especially valuable as a measure of under-nutrition, because at low levels of BMI there is less variation in muscle, bone and fat, since, all three compartments have been depleted to arrive at the low value. In contrast, high levels of BMI can be reached as a result of varying amounts of muscle, bone and fat and thus one cannot discern the composition of the increased mass relative to height. Thus, although BMI is correlated with fatness, it has limited ability to detect adiposity because of its failure to detect obesity (lack of sensitivity) in 20% to 50% children who are obese when measured by more direct methods (Lohman and Going, 2006).

Also, longitudinal measurements of BMI cannot discriminate relative changes in fat and lean mass. Nor does it give any information regarding the location of fat. In obese children, increases in activity may promote both gains in lean mass and loss of fat stores, resulting in weight maintenance. BMI may be particularly misleading in hospital patients, where children apparently "malnourished" in terms of BMI actually have an increase in relative body fat and a severe decrease in lean tissue. This may be important for their nutritional management, as the low BMI may lead to inappropriate overfeeding (Wells and Fewtrell, 2006).

Racial and ethnic differences in the composition of weight per unit height also confound interpretation of BMI. Several studies have shown significant racial or ethnic differences in body composition especially in bone and muscle mass (Wells and Fewtrell, 2008). BMI, thus, has significant limitations. Nevertheless, because of its simplicity and correlation with adiposity, BMI has become the preferred method (Maynard et al, 2001).

Fatfold thickness

Fatfold thickness has most of the characteristics of a good field method. The measurement is simple and quick, the calipers are inexpensive and portable and good reference data exists. Fatfolds are generally regarded as of low precision but proper training and continuous quality control prove the method to be acceptable (Norgan, 2005).

This technique for the estimation of body composition utilizes measurements of fatfold thickness at various anatomic sites. The use of fatfolds to estimate percent fat and indirectly fat free mass in children and adults is one of the most common and well established laboratory and field techniques. Many studies as well as national nutrition surveys have included fatfolds along with height and weight to better describe changes in body fat with growth and development.

Subcutaneous fat is measured using calipers that exert a standard pressure. The assumptions underlying this technique are; first that the thickness of the subcutaneous fat at the selected sites is representative of the total body fat and second, that the sites chosen for the measurement, either singly or in combination, represent the average thickness of subcutaneous fat (Lukaski, 1987; Brodie et al, 1998). The most commonly used method involves measurement at four sites: triceps, biceps, subscapular and suprailiac. These fatfold measurements when applied to race, age and sex specific prediction equations give information on the amount of fat in the body (Kurpad, 2003). In addition to total fat, it is also possible to assess the distribution of fat especially if circumferential measurements (mid upper arm, waist and hip circumferences) are also measured. As the method relies substantially on a limited number of fatfold sites, any differences in adipose tissue distribution from the original validated equation will impact on the prediction. In other words, the validity of using fatfold equations to predict body composition is restricted to populations from whom these equations were derived. It is essential that equations using fatfold data are cross-validated on other samples from the same and other populations to determine its general applicability. There has been little validation of the technique in obese subjects (Jebb and Wells, 2005).

The accessibility of the subcutaneous fat layer and the non-invasive nature of the technique has lead to the development of numerous equations for the prediction of body composition, using fatfold measurements as part of the equation. Most of these equations estimate body density, although some directly predict body fat

(Brodie et al, 1998). Population specific equations have been produced for many groups including infants (Oakley et al, 1977), college students (Durnin and Rahaman, 1967; Wilmore and Behnke, 1970), boys and girls separately (Brook, 1971) and pre-menarcheal and post-menarcheal girls (Young et al, 1968). Some equations use a combination of two fatfolds while others are based on four fatfolds. Nelson and Nelson (1986) reported that the best predictor of fat was a combination of triceps and subscapular. Some of the equations available for children and adolescents have been listed in Table 2.5.

However, one of the greatest drawbacks of this method is the poor reproducibility of the technique between different observers. The coefficient of variation (CV) for measurements made in six non-obese individuals by six experienced observers was 11%, 16%, 13% and 18% for triceps, biceps, subscapular and suprailiac, respectively, although when summed and translated into body fat the CV was only 4.6% (Fuller et al, 1991). In obese people, there are specific problems; the subcutaneous fat may be too large for the jaws of the calipers and it is difficult to locate the correct anatomical site than in lean individuals. Large subcutaneous fat deposits tend to be very compressible and so the measured thickness may vary with the time taken to make the measurement, which may impair the precision even further. Odema can lead to an overestimation of body fat, partly because the thickness of fatfold may be increased, but also because of increased body weight. Also, this measurement can be very distressing to some obese subjects as it makes a direct measure of their overt fat stores (Jebb and Wells, 2005). Although widely used in laboratory and field settings, clearly the accuracy or precision of fatfold measurement is dependent upon the skill of the investigator and the site measured (Pollock and Jackson, 1984); not all those who get trained develop the needed accuracy. Hence, it is not feasible in large scale surveys. This has somewhat limited the widespread application of anthropometry. Attempts were made to develop a method, which could help in assessment of body fat in large surveys. The most widely used alternative technique for the assessment of body composition in children is BIA.

Table 2.5: Prediction equations based on fatfold thickness for children and adolescents

Author, year	Equation	Description of the study
Durnin and Rahaman, 1967	Predicted density (kg/l): Boys = 1.1533 - 0.0643 x (log sum of 4 fatfolds) Girls = 1.1369 - 0.0598 x (log sum of 4 fatfolds)	These equations were derived from empirical relationships between fatfold thickness and body density in adolescents (48 boys age range 12.7-15.7 years; 38 girls age range 13.2-16.4 years).
Brook, 1971	Predicted density (kg/l): Boys = 1.1690 - 0.0788 x (log sum of 4 fatfolds) Girls = 1.2063 - 0.0999 x (log sum of 4 fatfolds)	These equations were derived from TBW and body density, in a sample of 13 obese children and 10 with short stature, age range 1-11 years. The equations are widely used in UK.
Johnston et al, 1988	Predicted density (kg/l): Boys = 1.1660 - 0.007 x (log sum of 4 fatfolds) Girls = 1.144 - 0.060 x (log sum of 4 fatfolds)	These equations are based on empirically derived relations between fatfolds and density of Canadian children aged 8-14 years (140 boys, 168 girls).
Slaughter et al, 1988	BF% for children with triceps and subscapular fatfolds <35 mm: Boys = 1.21 (sum of 2 fatfolds) – 0.008 (sum of 2 fatfolds)^2 -1.7 Girls = 1.33 (sum of 2 fatfolds) - 0-013 (sum of 2 fatfolds)^2 -2.5	These equations are based on an multicomponent method utilizing measurement of body density, TBW, and bone mineral content of radius and ulna. The sample used to derive these particular equations consisted of 50 boys (mean age 9.8 years) and 16 girls (mean age 10.0 years) from USA.
Deurenberg et al, 1990	Predicted density (kg/l) *(prepubertal)*: Boys = 1.1133 - 0.0561 x (log sum of 4 fatfolds) + 1.7 (age x 10^{-3}) Girls = 1.1187 - 0.0633 x (log sum of 4 fatfolds) + 1.9 (age x 10^{-3}) Predicted density (kg/l) *(pubertal)*: Boys = 1.0555 - 0.0432 x (log sum of 4 fatfolds) + 3.8 (age x 10^{-3}) Girls = 1.1074 - 0.0552 x (log sum of 4 fatfolds) + 1.6 (age x 10^{-3}) Predicted density (kg/l) *(post pubertal)*: Boys = 1.1324 - 0.0410 x (log sum of 4 fatfolds) Girls = 1.1830 - 0.0796 x (log sum of 4 fatfolds)	These equations are derived on 378 Dutch children aged 7-20 years. According to their maturational level they were divided into a prepubertal, a pubertal and a post pubertal group. The equations are widely used.
Goran et al, 1996	FM = 0.23 x subscapular + 0.18 x weight + 0.13 x tricep - 3.0	This equation was derived on 73 prepubescent children, 4-10 year old.

BIA

BIA equipment is portable, technique is non invasive and can be readily learnt by investigators (NIH, 1996). This method rests on the principle that fat is a poor conductor of an applied current, whereas fat free tissue, with its water and electrolyte content, is a good conductor. A small current is passed through the body to measure the body impedance, which is proportional to the conducting volume i.e. body water (Hoffer et al, 1969). The technique involves attaching adhesive surface electrodes to specific sites on the dorsal surface of hand and anterior surface of foot of the subject who lies flat on a non-conducting surface with legs abducted, preferably with thighs not touching, although this may not be possible in extremely obese subjects. The applied current is usually in the order of 500 µA for single (50 kHz) frequency machines, or 500 µA to 1 mA for multifrequency machines (5 kHz to 1 mHz), and tests times may last from a few seconds for a single frequency scan to several minutes for a full frequency scan (Brodie et al, 1998). The raw outputs are generally visible immediately on the analyzer (resistance and reactance), and subsequently transmitted to a host computer whereby dedicated software processes the data. At high frequencies, typically 50 kHz, the current is able to overcome the capacitance of cell membranes and fully penetrate the cells, giving a measure of TBW, whereas at low frequencies, for example 1 kHz, it cannot enter the cells and hence measures only extracellular water (Brodie et al, 1998). TBW measured is then converted into estimates of body fat and FFM, assuming a standard hydration fraction.

Traditionally, impedance was measured using a tetrapolar system with electrodes placed on the hand and foot. A new generation of equipment measures impedance from foot to foot (Jebb and Wells, 2005). Foot-foot measurements, though easier to obtain, have slightly poorer accuracy than whole body measurements (Parker et al, 2003). At present there are a host of commercial impedance machines available. The cost is generally related to the associated software, which may also make predictions of basal metabolic rate (BMR), total energy expenditure etc., based on additional measures of height, weight, gender, physical activity etc which are inserted into the programme. To maintain regression data accuracy, interchanging processing software from different manufacturer analyzers should be avoided (Brodie et al, 1998).

BIA has been shown to be highly reliable over repeated trials and for repeated measurements within a day and over several days or weeks for inter-observer and intra-observer comparisons with standardized measurement techniques. Although the resistance measurements obtained from BIA can be reliably measured with standardized technique, several factors affect impedance measures, including instrumentation, electrode placement, hydration status, food intake, exercise and temperature (Houtkooper et al, 1996).

Bioelectrical impedance analyzers of sound theoretical and well-engineered construction and containing precision parts are crucial to reliable body composition assessment. Baumgartner et al (1990) recommended that impedance measurements be made with the same type of analyzer used in developing the prediction equation to be applied. Deurenberg et al (1989) reported that resistance values differed by as much as 21 ± 5 Ω in a group of subjects measured under identical conditions but with two different impedance instruments that were the same model from one company.

The positioning of body and electrode placement also affects impedance measurements (Houtkooper et al, 1996). Surface electrodes were placed on the right side of the body on the dorsal surfaces of hand and foot (2 on each) proximal to the metacarpal-phalangeal (hand) and metatarsal-phalangeal joint (foot), and also medially between the distal prominences of the radius and ulna and between the medial and lateral malleoli at the ankle. The subject lies in supine position on a non-conducting surface with arms slightly abducted from the trunk, and with legs separated so that they are not in contact with each other

(Lukaski, 1987). The greater the separation of arms from the trunk, the higher will be the resistance values. Abducting the arm on which the electrodes are attached from 30° to 90° can result in 2% increase in resistance (Houtkooper et al, 1996). If the source and detector electrodes are placed closer than 4-5 cm, electrode polarization may occur and increase resistance (Baumgartner et al, 1990). A distance of 3 cm has been shown to be the minimum required for sufficient separation of the electrodes (Walker et al, 1990).

Making resistance measurements 2-4 hours after a meal decreases resistance values by as much as 17 Ω (Deurenberg et al, 1988). Fogelholm et al (1993) recommended an overnight fast as a routine standardization technique before impedance measurements. However, other investigators reported that food intake within 2 hours before measurement did not affect resistance values (Rising et al, 1991).

Fluid intake of 1.2-1.8 L of an oral rehydration solution was shown to increase resistance values, however, drinking 0.7-1.0L of water, oral hydration solution or diet soda did not affect resistance in studies by Rising et al (1991). Dehydration due to water loss during exercise has been reported to lead to a decrease in measured resistance (Khaled et al, 1988). Exercise of moderate intensity before impedance measurements does not affect resistance values but strenuous exercise before measurements results in a decrease in resistance values (Garby et al, 1990; Deurenberg et al, 1988).

Garby et al (1990) showed that a change in ambient temperature from 24°C to 34°C did not affect resistance values. Caton et al (1988) reported that taking impedance in warm (35°C) compared with cool (14°C) conditions results in a decrease in resistance values and overestimation of mean values for FFM (2.2 kg) and TBW (2.5 L).

Table 2.6: Prediction equations based on BIA for children and adolescents

Author, year	Equation	Description of the study
Davies et al, 1988	TBW = 0.60 × (ht^2 / impedance) + 0.50 (ht in m)	Twenty six healthy children aged 5-17 yrs were examined. The formula was validated using deuterium dilution.
Houtkooper et al, 1989	FFM = 0.58 × (ht^2 / impedance) + 0.24 × wt + 2.69	Forty one girls and 53 boys aged from 10 to 14 years were examined. The formula was validated using anthropometry and deuterium dilution.
Deurenberg et al, 1989	FFM = 0.430 × 10^4 × (ht^2 / impedance) + 0.354 × wt + 0.9 × sex; (sex: 1 = male, 2 = female; ht in m)	The data were obtained from 73 healthy prepubertal children; 8-11 years.
Deurenberg et al, 1990	*Boys and girls aged from 7 to 9 years:* FFM = 0.640 × 10^4 × (ht^2 / impedance) + 4.83 *Girls from 10 - 12 and boys from 10 - 15 years:* FFM = 0.488 × 10^4 × (ht^2 / impedance) + 0.221 × wt + 12.77 × ht – 14.7 *Girls aged over 13 and boys aged over 16 years:* FFM = 0.258 × 10^4 × (ht^2 / impedance) + 0.375 × wt + 6.3 × sex + 10.5 × ht – 0.164 × age – 6.5 (sex: 1 = male, 2 =female; ht in m)	A total of 246 children aged from 7 to 25 years were examined by means of BIA, densitometry and anthropometry. Since the results depended closely on age, 3 age-groups were formed.
Deurenberg et al, 1991	FFM = 0.406 × (ht^2 / impedance) + 0.306 × wt + 0.0558 × ht + 0.56 × sex ; where boys=1; girls=2	These sex and age specific prediction equations were derived on 166 boys and girls aged 7-15 years.
Houtkooper et al, 1992	FFM = 0.61 × (ht^2 / impedance) + 0.25 × wt +1.31 (ht in cm)	Houtkooper and his colleagues developed this formula in comparison to anthropometry, densitometry and deuterium dilution on 25 schoolchildren aged from 10 to 14 years, and on 68 children aged from 11 to 19 years.
Kushner et al, 1992	TBW = 0.593 × (ht^2 / impedance) + 0.065 × wt + 0.04 (ht in cm)	The measurements obtained from 116 subjects aged 0.02 months-67 years (62 adults, 37 prepubertal children, 44 preschool children and 32 underweight premature infants) were validated with BIA and deuterium dilution.
Young and Sinha, 1992	%BF = 0.3981 × (ht^2 / impedance) + 0.3066 × wt + 0.0953 (ht -100) + 0.7414	% BF was estimated in 50 males and 50 females aged 8-21 years using densitometry and BIA.
Schaefer et al, 1994	FFM = 0.65 × (ht^2 / impedance) + 0.68 × age + 0.15 (ht in cm)	Developed on 112 healthy children aged 11.8 ± 3.7 years. The FFM was calculated from measurements of total body potassium using ^{40}K spectrometry
Wabitsch et al, 1996	TBW = 0.35 × (ht^2 / impedance) + 0.27 × age + 0.14 × wt – 0.12 (ht in m)	The formula was developed using 146 overweight children aged 12.7 ± 3.0 years. The formula was validated using deuterium dilution method.

ht: height, wt: weight

Other variables such as time of day, menstrual cycle phase and use of contraceptives have not been significantly associated with variation in whole-body impedance values. However, Deurenberg et al (1988) reported impedance to be lower 1 week before menstruation in comparison with one week after.

The absolute accuracy of impedance depends upon the prediction equation employed (Elia, 1992). The plethora of different population-specific prediction equations has tended to undermine confidence in the BIA technique and no prediction equation has gained widespread acceptance (Jebb and Wells, 2005). Prediction equations have been validated and cross-validated in children, youth, adults and elderly, in primarily white populations and to a very limited extent in other ethnic groups like Asians, black and native American populations. Table 2.6 summarizes some of the predictive equations available for children and adolescents (Houtkooper et al, 1996).

Bhat et al (2005) have proposed a predictive equation to calculate body fat from bioelectrical impedance measurements in middle aged Indian men. However, so far no equation for deriving body fat from BIA in children has been developed in India and validated against gold standards such as DEXA. Schoeller and Kushner (1991) report that future research should focus on efforts on cross-validating published equations to eliminate the least accurate and least precise equations rather than to continue to develop new equations.

Heitmann (1990) compared fatfold thickness measurements, impedance and BMI by developing new multivariate regression equations for all three methods by using a cross-validation approach. He showed that even if all three methods predicted mean body fat equally well, the impedance method had significantly lower variability of estimates, making it the most accurate of the simpler methods. Das et al (2003) also reported that BIA offers better estimates of body fat than BMI alone. It is more precise and has less observer error than fatfold thickness (Fuller et al, 1991).

Overall, BIA is a useful method for use in epidemiological surveys. With proper standardization of methods, instruments and subject preparation, this non-invasive body composition assessment approach can quickly, easily and relatively inexpensively provide accurate and reliable estimates of FFM and TBW in healthy populations.

2.6 METHODS OF MEASURING DISTRIBUTION OF BODY FAT

The distribution of fat in adults and, although less documented, in children is significant for the risk of later complications of obesity. As is seen consistently in studies of adults, a central pattern of fat distribution, or abdominal adiposity, is associated with adverse levels of classic cardiovascular risk factors, independent of total fatness or weight status than the female pattern of gluteal-femoral fat distribution in adults (Weststrate et al, 1989). Elevations in LDL and total cholesterol, triglycerides and insulin as well as lower levels of HDL are associated with more centralized fat patterning (Freedman et al, 1999).

Much of the current interest in laboratory based body composition research is thus, in developing regional or tissue specific methods (Elia et al, 2000). Imaging methods, CT MRI and DEXA, are proving useful in regional measures of body composition important in nutritional status such as muscle mass and abdominal adipose tissue deposits. Though, more accurate methods for assessing abdominal adiposity, all these methods require costly equipment meaning that their use is limited to clinical research setting (Wells and Fewtrell, 2006).

Lately, it has been established that most disturbances related to abdominal obesity have their onset during childhood (Moreno et al, 2001). Central obesity in children has been found to be associated with adverse homeostatic factors, as measured by fibrinogen and plasminogen activator inhibitor-1 (Steinbeck, 2005). This has led to waist circumference receiving attention as a proxy for fat distribution. However, measuring fatness by recording the thickness of subcutaneous fat i.e. fatfolds has a long history.

Several fatfold ratios have been used to assess the subcutaneous adipose tissue distribution (Moreno et al, 2001; Ketal et al, 2007). The ratios of triceps to subscapular, peripheral to truncal (biceps+triceps / subscapular+suprailiac) and trunk to total fatfolds percent [(subscapular+suprailiac / biceps+triceps+subscapular+suprailiac)*100] have been used as indices of subcutaneous body fat distribution in children.

Savva et al (2000) reported waist circumference to be the most significant predictor for all cardiovascular risk factors, with BMI having a much lower predictive value. In another study, waist circumference correlated strongly with regional DEXA as compared to other anthropometric measures of abdominal adiposity (Daniels et al, 2000). Higgins et al (2001) suggested that children with 33% or more body fat and a waist circumference of 71 cm or more are likely to have an adverse cardiovascular risk profile. At present, there are no accepted cut-off points for waist circumference in children and adolescents, although some reference data for waist circumference in children and adolescents are available from several countries (Martinez et al, 1994; Zannolli and Morgese, 1996; Moreno et al, 1999; McCarthy et al, 2001; Katzmarzyk, 2004). As a result waist circumference is not measured as a part of routine screening. The recent International Diabetes Federation (IDF) definition of the metabolic syndrome in children includes waist circumference as mandatory criterion along with two or more other risk variables (Zimmet et al, 2007; Misra and Khurana 2008). Based on evidence from several studies (Bloch et al, 1987; Maffeis et al, 2001; Ford et al, 2005; Ng et al 2007), the IDF workshop has recommended the use the 90th percentile of waist circumference for defining obesity.

The problem with waist circumference for defining obesity and overweight is the lack of consensus over what defines the waist. The following, illustrated in Figure

2.4, are only some of the definitions. These different waist definitions give different results.

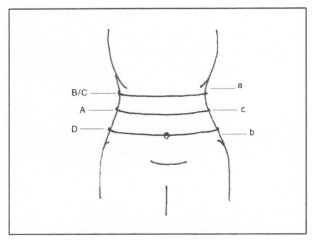

Figure 2.4: Various definitions of waist circumference measurements (Landmarks: a, lower border of costal margin in midaxillary line; b, upper border of iliac crest in midaxillary line; c, horizontal plane midway between a and b.

[A] The horizontal circumference at a level halfway between the lower border of the ribs in the mid axillary line and the upper border of the iliac crest in the same vertical line measured at the end of expiration (WHO, 1995).

[B] The circumference of the body at the area of noticeable narrowing at the waist (Katzmarzyk, 2004).

[C] The shortest circumference between ribs and hips when breathing out (National Obesity Forum, 2007).

[D] The body circumference at the level of the umbilicus

Measuring waist circumference is a simple, quick and robust measure of abdominal fat. Whole body data may appear optimal, but in practice regional data may be more informative about clinical condition, as well as more accurate. In obesity, the main concern is central adiposity, so monitoring of waist circumference may provide a better indication of health risk and response to treatment, than whole body fatness.

2.7 OBESITY BASED ON BODY FAT AS A CRITERION

Although there is overwhelming interest in the measurement of obesity and the concern regarding the rapid increases in prevalence, no accepted definition of excess adiposity exists in children and adolescents. Ideally, the choice of the %BF cutoff should be based on health-related criteria. Unfortunately, the long term health outcomes for different amounts of adiposity at different ages have not been described (Sardinha et al, 1999). The four studies that have evaluated metabolic risk in relation to measures of %BF in children and adolescents aged 5-18 years (Williams et al, 1992; Dwyer and Blizzard, 1996; Washino et al, 1999; Higgins et al, 2001) have reported percentage fat cutoff values indicating elevated cardiovascular disease (CVD) risk ranging from 20-33% in boys and 23-35% in females (Table 2.7).

Table 2.7: %BF cutoffs based on CVD risk

Reference	n	Age	Method	Cut-off	
				Boys	Girls
Williams et al, 1992	3320	5-18 yrs	Σ 2FFT	25	35
Dwyer and Blizzard, 1996	1834	9-15 yrs	Σ 4FFT	20	30
Washino et al, 1999	1289	9 and 10 yrs	BIA	23	23
Higgins et al, 2001	87	4-11	DEXA	33	33
FFT: fat fold thickness					

The health related cutoffs proposed by Williams et al, 1992 have been widely used (Sardinha et al, 1999; Neovius and Rasmussen, 2008). Williams et al (1992) suggested a criterion of ≥25% body fat for boys and ≥30% for girls based on his findings that higher percentages of body fat significantly increased the prevalence of selected cardiovascular risk factors such as high levels of adverse lipoprotein ratios and elevated blood pressure in children and adolescents aged 5-18 years compared to their leaner counterparts. He used age adjusted, sex- and race-specific equations to estimate %BF from fatfold measurements. These cutoffs are not age specific and only exist for overweight or excess fatness, not obesity.

The results of Williams et al (1992) became the basis for standards, setting the healthy range of body fatness at 10-25% for boys and 17-32% for girls by Lohman and Going (2006). They recommended percent fat values greater than 30% for boys and 35% for girls to be used as cutoffs for screening obesity.

Recently, pediatric cutoffs have been proposed by McCarthy et al (2006) for Caucasian children. The authors created age and sex specific curves for % BF estimated by BIA (Tanita BC-418MA) in 5-18 year old Caucasian children. They used the term 'overfatness' to denote adiposity exceeding the 85th percentile and 'obesity' for %BF exceeding the 95th. 'Underfat' denoted adiposity below the 2nd centile. However, the relationship of these cutoffs to cardiovascular risk factors remains unclear.

2.8 FACTORS LEADING TO CHILDHOOD OBESITY

Apart from genetic factors, two factors primarily emerge to be important i.e. lifestyle and behavior changes. They are primarily responsible for a sustained imbalance between calories consumed and calories expended. Modern lifestyle associated with lack of exercise, sedentary lifestyles, excessive television viewing and calories dense foods, are among the identified contributors to the global obesity epidemic.

2.8.1 Physical inactivity

Epidemiological studies have shown a negative relationship between measures of physical activity and indices of obesity (Dipietro, 1995). In a study in India on 13 to 18 year old children, age adjusted prevalence of over-nutrition was 17.8% for boys and 15.8% for girls. The prevalence increased with age and was higher in lower tertiles of physical activity and in higher tertiles of socio-economic group (Ramachandran et al, 2002). Decline in physical activity in children as they increase in age has been well documented. Strauss et al (2001) reported that there was a significant decline in physical activity levels especially moderate and vigorous physical activity levels (measured using the motion detector) between ages 10-16 years, in a cross-sectional study of 92 children. Malina (2001) reported a decrease in physical activity during the transition from adolescence to adulthood. It is suggested that it could be critical to have preadolescent children maximize their exposure to various activities at a young age to enhance the likelihood that they will maintain participation in some of these activities in later years (Kurpad et al, 2004).

In school going children, physical activity is related to school curriculum, especially during the ages 8-15 years (Kurpad et al 2004). Gavarry et al (2003) showed that school days increased the habitual physical activity of children (assessed through heart rate monitoring over a seven day period and daily activity diary) compared to school free days in their study of 182 children between the ages of 6-20 years. In contrast to the observations on school going children and adolescents, in primary school children aged 7 to 10.5 years, the total amount of physical activity did not depend on the duration of physical education timetabled at school, as these children compensated by being active out of school (Mallam et al, 2003).

High burden of school work, emphasis on tuitions and academic competitiveness have also led to decreased participation in sports and other forms of physical activity. The time spent on homework by 6-9 year olds in United States increased from 44 minutes per week in 1981 to more than 2 hours in 1997; the corresponding estimates for 9-11 year olds were 2 hours and 49 minutes in 1981 and more than 3.5 hours per week in 1997 (Malina and Katzmarzyk, 2006).

Conflicting reports on differences in patterns of activity among male and female children occur in several studies, with some showing definite differences while others showing none. Strauss et al (2001) reported that before the age of 13 years, similar levels of physical activity were present in girls and boys, while after the age of 13 years, boys were significantly more active than girls. By contrast, in 4-11 year old children, no gender difference was observed in activity energy expenditure and total energy expenditure and in the physical activity level (Grund et al, 2000).

Obese children spend less time in physical activity, more time in sedentary activities and rest (Maffeis et al, 1996). Higher amounts of physical activity have the potential to protect against obesity through the maintenance of energy balance and thus prevention of accumulation of excess adipose tissue.

2.8.2 Sleep

Short sleep duration has been shown to be a risk factor for obesity in children (Agras et al, 2004; Kuriyan et al, 2007), through the modulation of hormones such as leptin and ghrelin (Speigal et al, 2004; Taheri et al, 2006). Leptin levels reflect the quantity of adipose tissue in the body and regulate energy balance within the body by suppressing appetite and stimulating energy expenditure. Ghrelin is formed in the gastric mucosa and is elevated during hunger but falls on eating (Meier and Gressner, 2004). It has almost the opposite effect on appetite to leptin thus adding to the effects of short sleep duration on appetite (Taheri, 2006).

The almost universal presence of television and the fact that most children watch television, DVDs or videos, perhaps in their bedrooms, until late at night is one of the reasons for the present epidemic rise in childhood overweight and obesity. Children with television sets in their rooms, spent less time in bed on weekdays and reported higher overall levels of being tired (Dennison et al, 2002; Davison et al, 2006). It is likely that increased television viewing could be associated with lower sleep duration. Among children and adolescents, reducing television viewing to a minimum of 1 to 1.5 hours per day is desirable, as is encouraging them to sleep for at least 9 hours a day (Kuriyan et al, 2007)

2.8.3 Television viewing

Studies from several countries, including the USA, UK, Mexico, Thailand, New Zealand and Australia, have shown that the prevalence of obesity correlates with the time children spend watching television (Robinson et al, 1993; Gortmarker et al, 1996; Hernandez et al, 1999; Wake et al, 2003; Hancox and Poultan, 2006). Hancox et al (2004) reported that time spent watching television was a more significant predictor of BMI than diet or physical activity. The epidemic rise in childhood obesity in UK has roughly paralleled rises in the number of hours television programmes are available, the number of channels available and the opportunities to watch DVDs and videos as well as television. Dietz and Gortmaker (1985) estimated that the prevalence of obesity amongst 12-17 year old boys increased by 2% for every additional hour of television view per day.

Time spent watching television could be displacing more active pastimes and encouraging snacking. In urban areas, lack of appropriate play area and limited open space around home along with heavy traffic make it difficult for children to stay physically active and as a result they are forced to indulge in indoor games or watch television (Laxmaiah et al, 2007; Bhardwaj et al, 2008).

Advertising on television may also influence dietary habits and meal skipping; rushing meals seems more common in adolescents who watch more television. High levels of television viewing seem to be associated with greater consumption of high fat, high sugar, high salt (HFSS) foods in meals and snacks and less fruit and vegetables (Coon et al, 2001; Coon and Tucker, 2002). A report showed that by decreasing a child's television viewing by 7 hours a week, the risk of obesity is reduced by more than 30% (Crespo et al, 2001).

2.8.4 Excessive fat and sugar intake

Studies indicate that developing countries are using their growing incomes to replace their traditional diets that are rich in fiber and grain with diets that include a greater proportion of fat, salt and caloric sweeteners (Drewnowski and Popkin, 1997). The availability, convenience and low price of fast foods and pervasive influence of advertising for fast foods coupled with high population exposure to both media promotion and fast food restaurants are environmental variables contributing towards the epidemic of obesity (French et al, 2000). He associated more frequent fast food restaurant use with younger age, being unmarried, heavier body weight and having high BMI. Increase in frequency of fast food restaurant use was also associated with increase in total energy intake, percent energy from fat, servings of hamburgers, french fries and soft drinks (all energy dense foods) and less consumption of fruits and vegetables (Jeffrey, 2000). Kuriyan et al (2007) demonstrated that the increased consumption of fried and high fat foods were significantly associated with overweight among 6-16 year old children from Bengaluru and recommended reducing the frequency of eating fried and high fat foods to a minimum of 2-3 times per week. Similar results were seen in a previous study on children aged 9-14 years, where the higher consumption of fried foods from outside home was associated with greater total energy intakes, poorer diet quality and excessive weight gain (Taveras, 2005).

Harnack et al (1999) studied the trends in beverage consumption among children and adolescents and found that soft drinks, which are a source of empty calories, replace more nutritious beverages such as milk and fruit juices. A meta-analysis of 88 studies by Vartanian et al (2007) confirmed clear associations of soft drink intake with increased energy intake and body weight. China, India, Vietnam, Thailand and other South East Asian countries are currently major growth markets for soft drink industry (Malhotra and Siddhu, 2002). Diets high in sugar have also been associated with various health problems like dental caries, dyslipidemia, bone loss and fractures and poor quality diet (Johnson and Fray, 2001).

Thus, obesity is without doubt a critical public health concern and makes the prevention of childhood obesity a priority for all health professionals. Children should be the priority targeting population for prevention and intervention policy. Strategies for the prevention and management of overweight and obesity are basically simple enough, but an integrated approach at all levels i.e family, school and community is needed for sustainable motivation to remain normoweight. The first step in prevention and control of obesity is screening for overfat by field level techniques for early interventions. The present study is a small step in this direction.

3.0 METHODOLOGY

The present study was carried out on 6-14 year old affluent school going children to assess the prevalence of under/over-nutrition and to determine the amount and distribution of body fat. This was assessed anthropometrically and adiposity was assessed by both anthropometry and BIA.

3.1 SELECTION OF SUBJECTS

The subjects were boys and girls between the age groups of six to fourteen years studying in selected public schools in South Delhi. These subjects belonged to affluent families of professionals, high officials and businessmen. The major reason for considering subjects from high socioeconomic strata was that adiposity is likely to be more prevalent among affluent sections of the population than the poorer sections.

All the children from class I to IX, present on the day of data collection were enrolled for the study and height, weight, mid upper arm (MUAC), waist and hip circumferences, biceps, triceps, subscapular and suprailiac fatfold thicknesses were measured using standard techniques. A total of 3686 students (1898 boys, 1788 girls) participated in the study (Figure 3.1).

Body fat assessment using BIA was performed on a subset of 1220 subjects (667 boys, 553 girls) from the total number of 3686 subjects enrolled for the study (Figure 3.1). The amount of body fat was then assessed by two techniques; fatfolds and bioimpedance measurements. Four fatfold thicknesses i.e. triceps, biceps, subscapular and suprailiac were measured as a part of the anthropometric assessment. BIA test was carried out in the morning (2-3 hrs fasting) before lunch break after the subject had emptied bladder. Children who reported food intake or fluid intake within 1 hr before the measurement and girls who were menstruating or were expected to start their menstrual cycle within a week were excluded from the study.

Physical activity pattern and food habits were studied on a small sub sample of 81 subjects with high and low BMI.

Figure 3.1: Study design

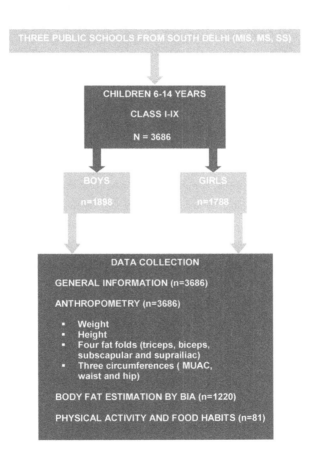

3.2 LOCALE

Children from three public schools in South Delhi- Mother's International School, Aurobindo Marg (classes I-IX, boys and girls), Modern School, Vasant Vihar (classes VI-IX, boys and girls) and Springdales School, Dhaula Kuan (class II girls) were enrolled to get the desired sample size. These schools were chosen because these were fairly representative of the urban affluent population of Delhi and the total strength of children per class was ample to obtain sufficient sample for statistically meaningful conclusions. In addition, these schools were conveniently located and easily accessible to the investigator and had an independent health centre for carrying out anthropometric and BIA measurements.

Of the three schools chosen, annual health checkup of students was carried out in two schools at the clinic/health centre located inside the school and information on general health of the students was entered in health cards. These cards were filled with the help of school doctor and records were maintained. The health cards were also distributed to parents in Parent-teacher meetings; the objective was to create awareness amongst the guardians about their wards overall health with special emphasis on over and under-nutrition. The investigator worked in collaboration with school health clinic and measured anthropometric indices and performed BIA on children who came for routine health check-up.

The third school did not have an ongoing health checkup system so measurements were taken in a separate room.

BIA was done at two schools which had the essential infrastructure i.e. an enclosed room with a wooden bed for the child to lie down and rest for 10 minutes before taking the readings.

A written consent for conducting the study was obtained from the Principals after clearly specifying the objectives of the study. The study protocol was discussed with the school Principals, who agreed to include height, weight, MUAC, waist and hip circumferences, biceps, triceps, subscapular and suprailiac fatfold thicknesses and BIA as a component of the existing school health check up for students.

3.3 SAMPLING TECHNIQUE AND SAMPLE SIZE

The present study is a cross-sectional study on 6-14 year boys and girls from three public schools in New Delhi to assess the prevalence of under/over-nutrition and the amount and distribution of fat. A total of 3686 subjects studying in classes I-IX were enrolled who reported to the health centre on the day of data collection. The purposive sampling technique was used to select the school. A list of eligible schools was prepared and then approached by the investigator to seek their participation in the study. The eligibility criteria for purposive sampling of schools were:

1. The principal should give consent.
2. The school should cater to primarily affluent children although some less affluent children may also be enrolled in school.
3. The school should have adequate sample of boys and girls in each age category.
4. The school should have separate medical centre for measurements and support staff to coordinate
5. The school should be conveniently located and accessible to the investigator for follow up.

Assuming that the prevalence of over-nutrition is about 30% (as assessed by BMI-for-age), the sample size required was estimated to be 200 per age for each sex. BIA was to be carried out on a sub sample, 50 subjects per age for both boys and girls, and the results were compared with fat mass values derived from anthropometry using fatfolds. The power of the study was set at 90% with an ά level of 0.05.

3.4 PERIOD OF DATA COLLECTION

The data was collected during the years 2004-2007 during the school timings.

3.5 AGE PROFILE

Age was calculated as age at the time of examination when the anthropometric data were recorded. Information regarding the date of birth of the subject was taken from the school records. The date of birth was subtracted from the date of examination to get the age of the subject in complete years and months. Age categories with the interval of one year were formulated. The whole data was arranged in nine age groups. All the subjects between ages 6.00 to 6.99 years were included in age group 6+, 7.00 to 7.99 years in the age group 7+ and so on up to 14 years. If a subject were six years twelve months and one day old, he or she was placed in the next age category of 7-7.99 years.

3.6 TOOLS AND TECHNIQUES FOR DATA COLLECTION

Table 3.1 presents the summary of tools and techniques used in the present study for data collection. The details of data collection are discussed below.

Table 3.1: Summary of tools and techniques used for data collection		
S. No.	DATA COLLECTED	TOOLS AND TECHNIQUES USED
1.	General information	Oral questionnaire
2.	Anthropometric measurements	
	• Weight	Seca Electronic Scale 890
	• Height	Microtoise
	• Circumferences -MUAC -Waist and hip circumference	PVC Fiber Glass Vernier Tape
	• Fatfold measurements -Biceps -Triceps -Subscapular -Suprailiac	Holtain's Calipers
3.	Techniques for body fat estimation	
	• BIA	Bodystat 1500 MDD Monitoring unit
	• from fatfold thicknesses	Using published equations
4.	Physical activity and food habits	Interview schedule

3.6.1 General information

A pretested oral questionnaire technique was used to elicit the general information from the subjects. A questionnaire was designed to collect information from each subject about date of birth of the subject, birth order, family size and occupation of the parents. The questionnaire was pretested on twenty five subjects in different age groups and then suitably modified after analyzing the response elicited during pretesting. The proforma finally used in the study is given in Annexure 1.

3.6.2 Anthropometric measurements

Training of the investigator: Standardized tools required for measurements including electronic weighing balance (Seca electronic scale 890), microtoise for height measurement (UNICEF, Copenhagen, Denmark), fibre glass tape with a vernier tape for circumferential measurements, Holtain's calipers for measurement of fat fold thickness, instrument for BIA measurement (Bodystat Analyzer for assessment of body fat using bioelectrical impedance technique) were procured prior to the initiation of the study. The investigator then underwent one week training for anthropometric data collection at the National Institute of Nutrition (NIN), Hyderabad.

The following anthropometric parameters were measured using the standard tools and techniques (Table 3.2) and the Proforma used for recording the anthropometric measurements is given in Annexure 2.

Table 3.2: Anthropometric parameters measured on study subjects and its sensitivity

Parameter	Tool	Sensitivity
Weight	Electronic seca scale	Nearest 100gm
Height	Microtoise	Nearest mm
MUAC	Fiber glass vernier tape	Nearest mm
Waist and hip circumference	Fiber glass vernier tape	Nearest mm
Fat folds (triceps, biceps, subscapular, suprailiac)	Holtain's Calipers	Nearest mm

Weight: Weight is an important anthropometric measurement used to assess body mass. It is the key anthropometric measurement indicator of current nutritional status (Jelliffe et al, 1989). Weight to the nearest 100g was recorded using *Seca electronic scale 890*. The subjects were weighed barefoot and with minimum clothing (Jelliffe et al, 1989). The weighing scale was calibrated with standard weights on a daily basis.

Height: Height reflects past nutritional status. Height was measured to the nearest mm by using a *wall mounted Microtoise*. Subjects were made to stand barefoot on a flat floor with weight distributed evenly on both feet, heels together, calfs, buttocks, shoulders and head in one straight line touching the wall. The legs were straight and shoulders relaxed. The head was positioned in frankfurt plane i.e. the upper border of the external auditory meatus was on a horizontal plane with the lower border of the eye. An upward pressure was exerted on the mastoid processes to facilitate erect position. The movable headboard was brought onto the topmost point on the head with sufficient pressure to compress the hair. The subjects were asked to look straight at their eye level and the reading was noted to the nearest 0.1 cm.

Comparison of the weight and height percentiles of boys and girls in the present study was made with two international references; *CDC 2000* and *WHO* 2007 and prevalence of under and over-nutrition was documented. *CDC 2000* growth reference represents the revised version of the 1977 NCHS growth charts based on data from 5 nationally representative child growth surveys (NHANES) conducted in the period 1963-1994 and represent the combined growth pattern of artificial-formula-fed and breastfed infants in the United States. The *WHO Reference 2007* is a reconstruction of the 1977 National Center for Health Statistics (NCHS)/WHO reference. It uses the original NCHS data set (1977; 1-24 years) supplemented with data from the WHO child growth standards sample for under-fives (2006; 18–71 months).

BMI: Both weights and heights were used to calculate BMI, which was defined as the ratio of body weight to body height squared, expressed in kg/m^2.

Comparison of the BMI percentiles of boys and girls in the present study was also made with two international references; CDC 2000 and WHO 2007 and prevalence of under and over-nutrition was documented. Prevalence was also estimated using the international cutoff points given by Cole et al (2000) for body mass index for child overweight and obesity. These international BMI cut offs cover the age range 2-18 years and are based on the internationally accepted cutoff points for adult overweight and obesity (i.e. BMI of 25 and 30 kg/m^2) at 18 years, obtained by averaging data from six countries namely Brazil, Great Britain, Hong Kong, Netherlands, Singapore and United States.

MUAC: Mid upper arm circumference was taken on the left arm using a non-stretchable, flexible *PVC coated fiberglass graduated tape* to which a vernier was attached to one end of the tape (Figure 3.2). The subject was asked to stand erect. The left arm was folded at right angle at elbow, keeping close to the body. The distance from tip of the shoulder (acromion) and the tip of the elbow (olecranon process) was measured and keeping the tape in position, midpoint was marked horizontally with a pen. The arm was then straightened and placed by the side of the body hanging freely. The tape was gently, but firmly placed embracing the arm at the midpoint without exerting too much pressure on the soft tissues.

The vernier tape is effective in providing precise measurement. It is easy to use and thus helps in taking the measurement faster.

Figure 3.2: PVC coated fiberglass vernier tape

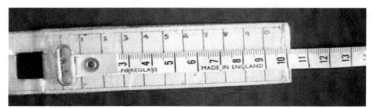

Waist and hip circumferences: In the recent past, particularly with increasing incidence of obesity, waist and hip circumferences are used to evaluate abdominal adiposity, which is associated with biochemical risk factors for cardiovascular diseases. Waist and hip circumferences were measured (to the nearest mm) by using a non-stretchable, flexible *PVC coated fiberglass graduated tape*, to which also vernier was attached to one end of the tape. The vernier tape improved both accuracy and ease in measurement, particularly in adolescents, as reading could be taken without getting too close to the subjects.

For waist measurement, subject was made to stand comfortably on a flat surface facing the observer, with weight evenly distributed on both feet and the feet about 25-30 cm apart. The tape was wound snugly at the lowest circumference between the costal margin and iliac crest (WHO, 1995) (see Figure 2.3). The circumference was obtained at the end of normal expiration. For hip (buttock) measurement, subject was asked to stand erect with arms at the side and feet together. The investigator sat at the side of the subject and placed the tape at the level of maximum extension of the buttock in a horizontal plane. The position of the tape on the opposite side of the subject's body was checked. The tape was fitted snugly against the minimum clothing of the subject but did not compress the soft tissues (Alexander and Dugdale, 1990). The measurement was recorded to the nearest 0.1 cm.

Waist circumference was compared with waist percentile charts given by Mc Carthy et al (2001) for 5-16.9 years old UK children.

Prevalence of abdominal obesity was determined using the International Diabetes Federation (IDF; 2007) cutoffs recommended for waist circumference. The new IDF definition is age specific, taking into account developmental challenges in growing children and adolescents (Table 3.3).

Table 3.3: The IDF consensus definition of the metabolic syndrome in children and adolescents

Age (yrs)	Obesity (WC)	Triglycerides	HDL-C	Blood pressure	Glucose (mm/liter) or known T2DM
6-<10	≥90th percentile	Metabolic syndrome cannot be diagnosed, but further measurements should be made if there is a family history of metabolic syndrome, T2DM, dyslipidemia, CVD, hypertension, and/or obesity			
10-<16	≥90th percentile or adult cutoff if lower[a]	≥1.7 mmol/liter (≥150 mg/dl)	<1.03 mmol/liter (<40 mg/dl)	Systolic ≥130/diastolic ≥85 mm Hg	≥5.6 mmol/liter (100 mg/dl) {if ≥5.6 mmol/liter (or known T2DM) recommend an OGTT}

[a] In adults central obesity is defined as waist circumference ≥94 cm for Europid men and ≥80 cm for Europid women, with ethnicity specific values for other groups

IDF: International Diabetes Federation; WC: waist circumference, HDL-C: high density lipoprotein cholesterol; T2DM: type 2 diabetes mellitus, OGTT: oral glucose tolerance test

Fatfold measurements: The fatfold measurement was taken at four sites using the *Holtain's fatfold calipers* with an accuracy of 0.2 mm. The measurement was made on the non dominant side of the body, by grasping skin and adjacent subcutaneous tissue between thumb and forefinger, shaking it gently to exclude underlying muscle, and pulling it away from the body far enough to allow jaws of the caliper to impinge on the skin. The jaws of the caliper compressed the tissues; caliper reading diminished for few seconds and then dial was read once the needle was in steady state.

The four sites measured were triceps, biceps, subscapular and suprailiac and the method of measurement according to WHO (1995) guidelines is explained below.

- **Triceps:** The measurement was taken on the dorsal side at the same midpoint where MUAC was measured. The vertical fold of the skin was held between the left thumb and index finger, one centimeter above the mid point, taking care not to include the underlying muscle. The caliper was held with right hand, horizontal to the ground and was pressed to open the contact surfaces. The caliper was applied to the fatfold and was released slowly so that the contact surfaces touch the middle of the fatfold. The reading was noted immediately as the subcutaneous fat gets compressed if the caliper is kept for a long time resulting in gradual decrease in the measurement.

- **Biceps:** The measurement was taken on the anterior side over the bicep muscles, one centimeter above the mid point where triceps was measured. The arm is placed by the side of the body hanging freely, with the palm of hand facing forward and a vertical pinch parallel to the long axis of the arm is made taking care not to include the underlying muscle.

- **Subscapular:** The fatfold is fairly uniform over this site. The fatfold was measured just below and lateral to the angle of the left scapula by picking it up with the thumb and forefinger in a line running approximately 45 degrees to the spine, following the natural fold of the skin.

- **Suprailiac:** The measurement was taken above the iliac crest (top of hip bone) on the most lateral aspect (side). The fold was directed anterior and downward in line with the natural fold of the skin.

Computed percentiles of triceps and subscapular fatfolds were compared with NHANES I (1971-74). Prevalence of obesity using triceps fatfold thickness was assessed using cutoffs proposed by Lohman and Going (2006) where boys with an estimated triceps fatfold thickness of 22 mm and girls with an estimated thickness of 27 mm were considered obese.

The peripheral to truncal (biceps+triceps/ subscapular+suprailiac) were used as indices of subcutaneous body fat distribution in boys and girls. The trunk to total fatfolds percent was also calculated.

3.6.3 Techniques to measure adiposity in children in field

The amount of fat (adiposity) was assessed using two field techniques:

- Anthropometry (multiple fatfolds) and
- BIA

which indirectly measure body density and body water respectively and their results were compared.

BIA was performed on a total of 1220 subjects. Fat fold data of these 1220 subjects was already collected as a part of anthropometric assessment. The Proforma used for recording BIA is given in Annexure 3.

Estimation of body fat from prediction equations based on anthropometry (multiple fatfolds) and BIA: Many race, age and sex specific equations have been published by several authors for the estimation of body fatness from anthropometry (multiple fatfolds) and BIA in children.

Inspite of the fact that there are good reasons to believe that the body fat and its distribution in Indian children may differ from the Caucasians, so far no equation for deriving fat mass from anthropometry (multiple fatfolds) or BIA have been developed in India and validated against gold standards such as DEXA. Because of this lacuna, fat mass was computed in the present study using available equations developed on Caucasian children.

Since age or maturational state has been identified as an important predictive variable of body composition (Reilly et al, 1995), therefore equations specific to the age range covered in the present study were selected.

[A] Body fat estimation from anthropometry (multiple fatfolds)

Two empirically derived child-specific equations were selected and applied to calculate fat mass (FM; in kg) and, subsequently, %BF from fatfold thicknesses. These were:

1. Equation by Slaughter et al (1988)

%BF for children with triceps and subscapular fatfolds <35 mm:

Boys = $1.21 (\Sigma 2SKF) - 0.008 (\Sigma 2SK)^2 + I$

Girls = $1.33 (\Sigma 2SK) - 0.013 (\Sigma 2SK)^2 - I$

%BF for children with triceps and subscapular fatfolds >35 mm:

Boys = $0.783 (\Sigma 2SK) + I$

Girls = $0.546 (\Sigma 2SK) + I$; where $\Sigma 2SK$= Sum of (triceps + subscapular); I =Intercept

Age wise intercepts (I)						
	Σ 2SK (mm)	6-9 yrs	10-11 yrs	12-13 yrs	14-15 yrs	16 yrs
Boys	< 35	-1.7	-2.5	-3.4	-4.4	-5.5
	> 35	2.2	0.6	0.6	-1.2	-1.2
Girls	< 35	2.5				
	> 35	9.7				

These equations were based on an empirically derived multicomponent method utilizing measurement of body density, total body water, and bone mineral content of radius and ulna. The sample used to derive these equations consisted of 242 subjects (66 prepubescent children, 59 pubescent and 117 postpubescent children) aged 6-18 years from USA. The cross validity of the Slaughter et al (1988) equations has been reported to be high (Janz et al, 1993).

2. Equation by Johnston et al (1988)

Predicted density (kg/l):

Boys= $1.1660 - 0.070$ (log sum of 4 fatfolds)

Girls= $1.144 - 0.060$ (log sum of 4 fatfolds)

These equations were based on empirically derived relations between fatfolds at four sites i.e. triceps, biceps, subscapular and suprailiac and body density of 8-14 years old (140 boys, 168 girls) Canadian children from public schools and separate schools. The prediction equation from fatfold measurements were derived from linear regression of body density vs the log of sum of fatfold thickness. Body fat percent was calculated using the following equation by Lohman et al (1984) calculated for prepubescent children, which takes into account the lower bone-mineral content and higher water content:

% BF = (5.30 / Density – 4.89)*100

The cross validity of these equations has not been reported.

[B] Body fat estimation from BIA

Whole body bioelectrical impedance analysis was carried out on the subjects using the *Bodystat 1500 MDD Monitoring unit*. The principle of estimating fat mass by bioimpedance is relatively simple. An electrical signal of known frequency is transmitted across a tissue bed and the impedance/resistance to this transmission is related to the conduction properties of the tissue. Electrolyte-containing fluids have relatively low impedance while tissues devoid of fluids have high impedance (Kushner, 1992).

This BIA device is tetrapolar (has four electrodes), which apply a current of 500 micro amps at a single frequency of 50 kHz. The 500 µA current that is supplied is not strong enough to be sensed by the subject. A specific Bodystat calibrator (500 Ω) was used daily to confirm the reproducibility of the measurements. BIA test was carried out in the morning (2-3 hrs fasting) after the subject had emptied bladder.

The subject was made to lie down in the supine position on a non-conducting surface (wooden bed) at least 50 cm away from any electrical devices and with no part of the body touching one another i.e. the arms slightly abducted from the trunk, and with legs separated so that they are not in contact with each other and the ankles were at least 20 cm apart. The head may be on a thin pillow or level. The subject was asked to remove his/her shoes, socks and any metallic objects like pens, coins, watch, belt, bracelets, earrings, anklets etc and lie still for atleast four to five minutes, so that all fluids are in equilibrium. The areas where electrodes were applied were first cleaned with spirit and left to dry. Electrodes were placed on the right side of the body on the dorsal surfaces of hand and foot (2 on each) proximal to the metacarpal-phalangeal (hand) and metatarsal-phalangeal joint (foot), and also medially between the distal prominences of the radius and ulna and between the medial and lateral malleoli at the ankle (Figure 3.3). The positioning of the body and electrode placement is important as they may affect impedance measurements. The right side was used in order to avoid stimulation of electrically excitable tissues such as cardiac muscles and nerves on the left side of the body. The device was then switched on and the impedance value calculated by the manufacturer's software was recorded.

Figure 3.3: Placement of the electrodes for BIA measurement

The BIA instruments come with an inbuilt equation for deriving fat mass and fat free mass from the impedance value. These equations have been usually derived from studies carried out in Caucasian populations. The BIA instrument used in the present study uses the equation given by *Houtkooper et al* (1992).

Fat mass was thus computed from impedance using the following equation worked out by Houtkooper et al (1992) for Caucasian children (as given in the manufacturer's software):

1. **Equation by Houtkooper et al (1992)**

   $FFM = 0.61*(Height^2 / impedance) + 0.25*weight + 1.31$

   Houtkooper et al (1992) determined FFM from body density (underwater weighing), body water (deuterium dilution) and from age-corrected density equations (anthropometry) on 25 school children aged from 10 to 14 years, and on 68 children aged 11 to 19 years. Prediction equations were developed using multiple regression analyses and cross-validated in three different samples. As a result of all cross-validation analyses, the above mentioned equation based on body water (deuterium dilution) was recommended.

   For comparison, three other child specific prediction equations from literature based on BIA that matched the age range of the present study subjects, namely Deurenberg et al (1991), Kushner et al (1992) and Schaefer et al (1994) were also applied to calculate fat mass.

2. **Equation by Deurenberg et al (1991)**

   $FFM = 0.406*(Height^2 / impedance) + 0.306*weight + 0.0558*height + 0.56*sex$
   where boys=1; girls=2

   These sex and age specific prediction equations were derived on 166 boys and girls aged 7-15 years. The cross validity of this equation has been reported to be high.

3. **Equation by Kushner et al (1992)**

   $TBW = 0.593*(Height^2 / impedance) + 0.065*weight + 0.04$

The equation was derived on 62 adults, 37 prepubertal children, 44 preschool children, and 32 premature low birth weight neonates and a single impedance equation for populations of various ages from infancy to adulthood i.e. 0.02 months to 67 years was developed.

4. Equation by Schaefer et al (1994)

$FFM = 0.65*(Height^2 / impedance) + 0.68*age (years) + 0.15$

This equation was developed on 112 healthy children from Germany aged 3.9-19.3 years. The FFM was calculated from measurements of total body potassium using ^{40}K spectrometry.

Overweight and obesity based on %BF: There are no reference standards for %BF in children. However, the commonly used %BF reference is the health-related %BF cutoffs proposed by Williams et al (1992). The cutoffs for %BF proposed by Williams et al (1992) have been coupled with a significant overrepresentation of cardiovascular risk factors. In a sample of 5-18 yrs old subjects who had their %BF estimated by fatfolds, they found that 25% body fat for boys and 30% body fat for girls respectively were suitable to define excess fatness. These cutoffs only exist for overweight (or excess fatness), not obesity and are not age specific.

Based on the work of Williams et al (1992), Lohman and Going (2006) recommended percent fat values greater than 30% for boys and 35% for girls to be used as cutoffs for screening obesity.

Percent fat derived from fatfolds were compared with norms from NHES fatfold data (1963-65) obtained using the fatfold equations from Slaughter et al (1988) as given by Lohman and Going (2006). FFM (kg) and %BF estimated from BIA for children aged 12-18 years were compared with data from NHANES III (Chumlea 2002).

[C] Validation of BIA with the deuterium dilution technique

Subjects: Validation of BIA was observed on seventeen subjects (6-15 years, both boys and girls) studying in a government school, at the to Institute of Population Health and Clinical Research, St John's National Academy of Health Sciences, Bengaluru.

The subjects reported to the laboratory at 0800 h empty stomach. The subjects completely evacuated the bladder to provide basal sample of urine. Each subject orally consumed deuterium oxide (D_2O, 99.9%, Europa Scientific, Crewe, UK) in a dose of 75mg/kg body weight, from sterile plastic containers with the aid of a straw followed by 50ml distilled water using the same straw. The containers were tightly sealed with the straw tightly crushed within it and post dose weight of the containers recorded, to calculate the exact amount of isotope consumed. Urine samples were collected half hourly from the fourth hour after dosing until the fifth hour, and stored at -20°C. The urine samples were then analysed for deuterium using a dual inlet Mass Spectrometer (Europa Scientific, Crewe, UK); the results are given in Annexure 4. The predictive equation derived from this dataset was:

FFM =0.222 + 0.481*(Height^2/impedance) + (0.406*weight) - 0.945* sex

where sex=1 for girls and 0 for boys

3.6.4 Physical activity pattern and food habits

Physical activity pattern and food habits was studied on 81 subjects, 34 under-nourished and 47 over-nourished as assessed by BMI-for age (CDC 2000) between the age range 8-10 years to ascertain the factors responsible both for under and over-nutrition among affluent school children. These children were placed in two groups on the basis of their BMI:
- Group O (>+2SD of the BMI-for-age CDC 2000; n=47) and
- Group U (<-2SD of the BMI-for-age CDC 2000; n=34)

Only prepubescent age group was taken as children smaller than this will not be able to recall correctly and older adolescents are vulnerable to faulty food habits.

Physical activity pattern: Information regarding the physical activity pattern for one working day was collected using an interviewer-administered questionnaire. Subjects were asked to recall all the activities performed during the previous working day in order to obtain some valid information regarding the habitual frequency and duration of different activities in school, games, travel, tuition, sedentary habits at home, household work, hobbies, exercise and sleep. Guidelines with respect to the recording of the activities are given in Annexure 5A.

Their habitual activities were grouped into 3 broad domains (Kuriyan et al, 2007), consisting of:
- Sedentary activities (all sedentary activities at school and home),
- Moderate to rigorous activities (physical training at school, games and exercise at and after school)
- Sleep

The duration of TV viewing was considered separately as an independent variable.

Prediction of BMR: BMR was calculated using the prediction equation given by FAO/WHO/UNU, 2004. The equation recommended for 8-10 year old boys and girls is as follows:

Boys (8-10 yrs): BMR (Kcal/day) = 22.706 * weight + 504.3
Girls (8-10 yrs): BMR (Kcal/day) = 20.315 * weight + 485.9

This was then expressed in Kcal/minute as follows:

BMR (Kcal/min) = BMR (Kcal / 24hr) / 1440

Calculation of total day's energy expenditure (TDEE): TDEE was calculated for one working day. For each reported activity a MET (metabolic equivalent), which is essentially a multiple of BMR was applied. Higher METs indicate higher levels of physical activity. METs were taken from two sources; Compendium values (Ainsworth et al, 1993) and FAO/WHO/UNU (2004) values (Annexure 5B). The total energy expenditure for a particular activity was thus computed as a product of the duration of that activity in minutes (d), the specific MET (m) and the BMR/min. The total 24-hr energy expenditure was computed by summation of the above {d x m x BMR} (Annexure 5B).

Food habits: Information on food habits like number of meals consumed, meal skipping pattern, canteen use and eating out pattern was also collected on these subjects using an interviewer-administered questionnaire. The questionnaire was pretested and after analyzing the responses elicited during pretesting, it was suitably modified. The questionnaire finally used in the study is given in Annexure 6.

3.7 SELECTION OF GOVERNMENT SCHOOL BOYS

In order to assess the magnitude of differences in anthropometry and body fat among boys from the public schools (catering to the affluent sections of the population) and government schools (catering to lower socioeconomic sections of the population), 9 year old boys studying in a government school located in the same geographical area as that of public schools i.e. South Delhi, were enrolled. Nine year old boys from class 3 to 5, present on the day of data collection were enrolled for the study and height, weight, mid upper arm, waist and hip circumferences, biceps, triceps, subscapular and suprailiac fat fold thicknesses and body fat using BIA were measured using standard techniques. A total of 90 boys from government school participated in the study.

For comparison with public schools, 108 boys, 9 year old, on whom all anthropometry i.e. height, weight, mid upper arm, waist and hip circumferences, biceps, triceps, subscapular and suprailiac fat fold thicknesses and body fat using BIA were measured, were included for this study. In order to obtain sufficient sample and statistically meaningful conclusions from comparison with government school boys, BIA was purposely done on more number of boys in the 9+ age group in public schools as compared to other age categories.

The anthropometric and body fat data of all government and public school boys (9 year old) is given in Annexure 7A and B respectively.

3.8 QUALITY CONTROL

Quality control was maintained in order to minimize intra-individual errors. Actual data collection began only after repeated quality control checks showed that the measurements were consistent and accurate. The quality control methods followed during the study are given below.

3.8.1 Quality control methods for equipments

Weighing balance was checked using standard weights. The microtoise was fixed permanently on one of the walls in the school (with minimum/no skirting), checked for its angle and position before taking the measurements and in case of any error was fixed properly again. A vernier scale was attached to the fibreglass tape for improving ease and accuracy. Bodystat analyzer was calibrated each day before taking the readings using a calibrator that comes with the analyzer.

3.8.2 Quality control methods for anthropometric measurements

As a routine, all anthropometric measurements were done in duplicate on approximately every 10th child. Data on such duplicate measurements is given in table and figure. Excellent concordance was there between duplicate measurements carried out in a randomly chosen child (Table 3.4). A similar exercise was done in a substantially small sample for BIA. Measurements were taken at a similar time point each day with limited physical exertion in an attempt to reduce measurement error. BIA was robust and so no significant difference was found. In view of this quality control it was possible to pool all the data collected over a three-year period in different schools and analyze the data.

Table 3.4: Standardization to remove intra-individual variation						
Parameter		A		B		p value
	n	Mean	SD	Mean	SD	
Weight	234	49.6	15.7	49.7	15.8	0.33
Height	190	146.9	18.2	146.9	18.2	0.18
MUAC	234	22.4	4.4	22.5	5.0	0.22
Triceps	234	12.7	7.1	12.7	7.1	0.87
Biceps	234	10.3	5.5	10.2	5.4	0.27
Supscapular	234	14.6	8.8	14.5	8.8	0.50
Suprailiac	234	15.9	8.6	15.9	8.2	0.08
WC	234	70.9	12.4	71.1	12.4	0.62
HC	234	85.4	13.9	85.7	14.4	0.25
NS, paired t-test						

3.9 STATISTICAL ANALYSIS

The data collected, both qualitative and quantitative, was consolidated and systematically tabulated. Analysis was done on Microsoft Excel and STATA SE 9.0

Mean, median, standard deviations and percentiles were calculated for each age category separately for boys and girls for all anthropometric indices i.e. weight, height, BMI, four fatfolds (triceps, biceps, subscapular, suprailiac), and three circumferences (MUAC, waist and hip) and % BF. Δweight, Δheight and ΔBMI per year were also calculated. The data on TDEE was also expressed as mean ± SD. The anthropometric data, body fat and energy expenditure related data were analyzed for difference in mean values using the Student's t-test and two-sample Wilcoxon rank-sum (Mann-Whitney) test.

Z-scores and smoothened percentiles were generated for boys and girls separately using the LMS method, which summarizes the data in terms of three smooth age-specific curves, namely L (lambda), M (mu) and S (sigma). The M and S curves correspond to the median and coefficient of variation for the variable at age where as L curve allows for substantial age dependent skewness of the variable. For the construction of z-score curves, lmsChartMaker Pro version was used.

Pearson's correlation coefficients (r) were calculated to assess relationships between:

- fat mass and different anthropometric measurements
- fat mass computed using BIA and fat mass computed from anthropometry
- BMI and %BF

Comparison of two techniques and to find the differences in estimates between two techniques was done using Bland and Altman statistical analysis (1986). A significant difference between the techniques was assessed by paired t-test.

Receiver operating characteristic (ROC) analysis was done to evaluate the accuracy of:

- BMI as an indicator of obesity as assessed by %BF
- MUAC, triceps and subscapular fatfold thicknesses and waist circumference as indicators of obesity as assessed by %BF as the criteria

With the use of %BF values, obese boys and girls who were classified correctly as obese by the anthropometric variables represent the true-positive cases, whereas obese subjects classified as non-obese represent false-negative cases. Non-obese subjects classified correctly as non-obese represent the true-negative cases, whereas non-obese subjects classified as obese represent false-positive cases.

Sensitivity of the anthropometric diagnosis is the probability that the anthropometric variables will classify a subject as obese when the subject is truly obese (true-positives); the specificity is the probability that the anthropometric variables will classify a subject as non-obese when the subject is truly non-obese (true-negatives). In the ROC analysis, true-positive rate (sensitivity) is plotted against the false-positive rate (1-specificity). The best tradeoff is the criteria value that maximizes the sum of sensitivity and specificity. Area under the curve (AUC) - the index reflecting the overall accuracy of the diagnostic test was also derived from the ROC analysis.

The level of significance for all analysis was set at $p < 0.05$.

4.0 RESULTS

There is very little data on body fat in school children. This is because of the problems in measuring fat. The present cross-sectional study was thus undertaken on 3686 subjects (1898 boys, 1788 girls) aged 6-14 years from three public schools of South Delhi catering to the urban affluent population of Delhi. Data collection included measurement of nine anthropometric parameters (height, weight, MUAC, waist and hip circumferences, triceps, biceps, subscapular and suprailiac fat fold thickness) of all the subjects. Body fat assessment using BIA was conducted in a selected sub sample of 1220 subjects, 667 boys and 553 girls.

The results are presented and discussed as follows:

4.1: General profile of the study population
4.2: Anthropometric profile of the study population
4.3: Body fat estimation
4.4: Physical activity pattern and food habits
4.5: Public school vs. government school boys (9 year old)

4.1 GENERAL PROFILE OF THE STUDY POPULATION

Information on the socio-demographic aspects of families to which subjects belonged is presented in this section. Questions pertaining to income status of the subjects had to be removed from the Proforma as the schools had objection and so this information could not be collected. The subjects belonged to well-to-do families of professionals, high officials and businessmen residing mostly in South Delhi.

4.1.1 Type of family

The type and size of the family are depicted in Table 4.1.1 A nuclear family is defined in NFHS-3 (2005-06) as a family that comprises of a married couple or a man or a woman living alone or with unmarried children (biological, adopted, or fostered), with or without unrelated individuals. According to this, the proportion of nuclear families was larger (59.1%) than the proportion of non-nuclear families (40.9%).

The mean family size was 4.7 persons per family as compared to 5.4 persons per family reported in NFHS-2 (1998-99), depicting a decline in family size. In the present study also, only 6.0% of families comprised of seven or more members depicting that the family size is shrinking.

Table 4.1.1: Type and size of the family

Type of family	n	Number of members in the family						
		3	4	5	6	7	8	9+
Nuclear	2179 (59.1)	458 (21.0)	1405 (64.5)	237 (10.9)	-	-	-	-
Non-nuclear	1507 (40.9)	-	86 (5.7)	359 (23.8)	841 (55.8)	142 (9.4)	74 (4.9)	6 (0.4)
Total	3686	458 (12.4)	1491 (40.4)	596 (16.2)	841 (55.8)	142 (3.9)	74 (2.0)	6 (0.1)

4.1.2 Number of children in the family

Table 4.1.2 shows that most (85.5%) of the nuclear families had up to two children and a small percentage (14.5%) had three children. Among the non-nuclear families 80.8% comprised of one or two children, while the rest (19.2%) had three to more than even five children. These 19.2% of non-nuclear families had two or more nuclear families residing together.

Table 4.1.2: Number of children in the family						
Type of family	Number of families	Number of children in the family				
		1	2	3	4	≥5
Nuclear	2179	458 (21.0)	1405 (64.5)	316 (14.5)	-	-
Non-nuclear	1507	230 (15.3)	987 (65.5)	210 (13.9)	77 (5.1)	3 (0.2)
Total	3686	688 (18.7)	2392 (64.8)	526 (14.3)	77 (2.1)	3 (0.1)

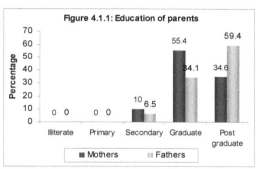

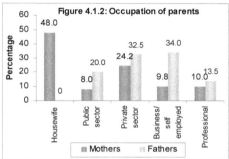

4.1.3 Education status of the parents

Information on the education level of the parents was available from 1677 subjects only and is depicted in the Figure 4.1.1. Majority of mothers (55.4%) were graduates and almost one third (34.6%) had done post graduation/ professional graduation like MBA, MCA, CA, engineering etc. A small proportion of mothers (10.0%) did not study beyond class XII.

Men had substantially higher educational attainment than women. Number of fathers with post graduation/ professional graduation (59.4%) almost doubled that of mothers who were post graduates (34.6%). None of the parents were illiterate.

4.1.4 Occupation of the parents

Figure 4.1.2 illustrates the occupation profile of the parents. Information regarding the occupation profile of the parents was available from 2647 subjects only. Almost half of mothers (48.0%) were housewives and were not employed outside their homes and the rest (52.0%) were working mothers. Upto 24.2% of the mothers were into private services mainly working with multinational companies while 8.0% were either teachers in public schools, colleges or were employed in government departments like railways, electricity board etc or working in banks.

Equal number of fathers were businessmen/self employed (34.0%) or into private services (32.5) mainly working with multinational companies. Others (13.5%) were professionals like doctors, architects, lawyers, chartered accountants, software professionals.

To sum up the socio-demographic profile of subjects in the present study:

- Most subjects came from nuclear families (59.1%). Non- nuclear families were 40.9%; 19.2% of non-nuclear families had two or more nuclear families residing together.
- The mean family size was 4.7 persons per family.
- Most (83.5%) of the families had upto two children.
- None of the parents were illiterate. Majority (55.4%) of mothers were graduates. Men had substantially higher educational attainment than women with 59.4% of fathers having a post graduation/ professional graduation degree.
- Almost half were working mothers (52.0%). Equal number of fathers were businessmen/self employed (34.0%) or into private services (32.5) mainly working with multinational companies.

4.2 ANTHROPOMETRIC PROFILE OF THE STUDY POPULATION

All children 6-14 years, boys and girls, studying in classes I-IX in selected public schools, present on the day of data collection were enrolled for the study and weight, height, three circumferences (MUAC, waist and hip circumferences) and four fatfold thicknesses (triceps, biceps, subscapular and suprailiac) were measured.

A total of 3686 subjects, 1898 boys and 1788 girls, were enrolled during the course of the study. The mean ages in both gender groups were fairly comparable for all the ages (Table 4.2.1). Data pertaining to each parameter including mean, standard deviation, median and (-2) SD and (+2) SD z-scores are presented in the following pages.

Table 4.2.1: Age and sex wise distribution of subjects

Age (yrs)	Boys	Mean age (yrs)	Girls	Mean age (yrs)
6+	214	6.5	200	6.5
7+	200	7.5	224	7.5
8+	212	8.5	202	8.5
9+	205	9.4	214	9.5
10+	201	10.6	201	10.6
11+	202	11.4	202	11.4
12+	205	12.5	170	12.5
13+	245	13.5	201	13.5
14+	214	14.4	174	14.4
Total	1898		1788	

4.2.1 Weight

Tables 4.2.2 and 4.2.3 depict the mean weight and Δ weight per year between 6-14 years of both boys and girls. Details regarding percentiles of weight for both boys and girls are given in Annexure 8A.

There was a progressive increase in weight with increase in age in both boys and girls (Tables 4.2.2 and 4.2.3). The girls were lighter than boys at most age points except at 10-12 years. In boys, a gradual increase in mean weight was seen between 11-13 years and the peak annual increase in weight (6.5 kg/year) was seen at 13+ years. In girls, peak increase in annual weight gain was seen between 10-12 years (over 6 kg/year) and it continued to remain high till 12+ years (Figure 4.2.1). At age 13+ years, the increase in weight per year was least for girls (0.9 kg/year) indicating cessation of rapid growth post puberty.

Our data is in line with the data from longitudinal studies in literature which also showed cessation of rapid growth among adolescent girls around 13 years. Such rapid dip in weight was not seen in boys; probably this is not evident in boys till 14 years and mostly occurs by 18 years (Tanner, 1989). The total gain in weight from age 10-14 years was 21.3 kg among boys and 12.6 kg among girls and at the age of 14+ years boys were heavier than girls by 6.8 kg.

Table 4.2.2: Weight (kg) of boys (n=1898)				Table 4.2.3: Weight (kg) of girls (n=1788)			
Age (yr)	n	Mean ± SD	Δ weight/yr	Age (yr)	n	Mean ± SD	Δ weight/yr
6+	214	23.9 ± 4.8	-	6+	200	23.9 ± 5.1	-
7+	200	27.1 ± 5.8	3.2	7+	224	26.7 ± 5.8	2.8
8+	212	30.3 ± 6.9	3.2	8+	202	29.8 ± 6.2	3.1
9+	205	33.5 ± 7.3	3.2	9+	214	33.4 ± 6.8	3.6
10+	201	37.9 ± 8.7	4.4	10+	201	39.8 ± 10.6	6.4
11+	202	42.9 ± 10.6	5.0	11+	202	43.9 ± 9.3	4.2
12+	205	48.4 ± 12.9	5.6	12+	170	49.3 ± 10.1	5.3
13+	245	55.0 ± 12.6	6.5	13+	201	50.2 ± 9.6	0.9
14+	214	59.2 ± 13.3	4.2	14+	174	52.4 ± 9.9	2.2

The weight trajectory in Figure 4.2.2 shows that the median weights of both boys and girls were comparable till the age of 12+ years, after which the median weights in boys continued to increase and were higher than weights of girls.

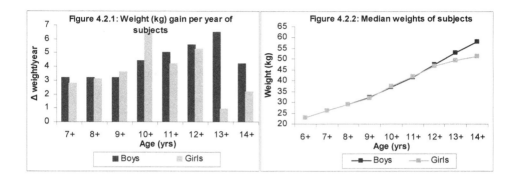

Figure 4.2.1: Weight (kg) gain per year of subjects

Figure 4.2.2: Median weights of subjects

[A] Comparison with international references

Comparison of the weight percentiles of boys and girls in the present study was made with two international references; CDC 2000 and WHO 2007. Prevalence of underweight and overweight was then estimated.

CDC 2000

The present study data and CDC 2000 reference data for weight of boys and girls are compared in Figures 4.2.3 and 4.2.4 and details are given in Tables 4.2.4 and 4.2.5 respectively.

Boys

There was a progressive increase in weights of boys up till 14+ years. The median and (+2) SD z-scores of boys were higher than the respective CDC 2000 z-scores for all ages, while the (-2) SD z-scores of boys and the corresponding CDC 2000 z-scores overlapped (Figure 4.2.3).

Table 4.2.4 shows that for the median curve, boys had weights higher than the CDC 2000 for all the ages, the difference being more distinct from 10+ years of age. At age 6+ years, boys were heavier by 1.2 kg as compared to the CDC 2000 data. The gap increased to 5.0 kg at the age of 14+ years. At (-2) SD level, boys had weights lower than that of CDC 2000, the difference being 0.7 kg at 14+ years. For (+2) SD curve at age 14+ years, boys were heavier by 10.4 kg as compared to the CDC 2000 data (Table 4.2.4).

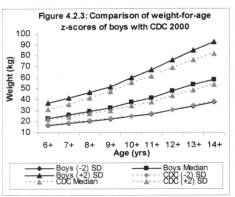

Figure 4.2.3: Comparison of weight-for-age z-scores of boys with CDC 2000

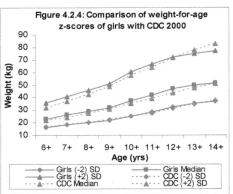

Figure 4.2.4: Comparison of weight-for-age z-scores of girls with CDC 2000

Table 4.2.4: CDC 2000 and present study (PS) weight-for-age (kg) z-scores for boys (n=1898)

Age (yrs)	(-2) SD		Median		(+2) SD	
	PS	CDC	PS	CDC	PS	CDC
6+	16.7	17.1	23.1	21.9	36.5	30.9
7+	18.5	18.8	26.0	24.3	41.3	35.7
8+	20.3	20.7	29.2	27.0	46.5	41.3
9+	22.1	22.5	32.4	29.9	51.8	47.0
10+	24.6	25.0	37.2	34.2	59.6	55.1
11+	26.9	27.1	41.6	37.7	66.7	61.0
12+	30.2	30.4	47.4	43.0	76.0	68.8
13+	33.8	34.1	53.1	48.3	84.6	75.7
14+	37.3	38.0	58.2	53.2	92.1	81.7

Table 4.2.5: CDC 2000 and present study (PS) weight-for-age (kg) z-scores for girls (n=1788)

Age (yrs)	(-2) SD		Median		(+2) SD	
	PS	CDC	PS	CDC	PS	CDC
6+	16.3	16.6	22.9	21.5	35.5	31.8
7+	18.2	18.3	26.1	24.1	40.8	36.8
8+	19.9	20.1	28.9	27.2	45.7	42.6
9+	21.7	22.1	31.8	30.6	50.7	48.7
10+	25.3	25.0	37.6	35.4	60.2	57.3
11+	28.4	27.5	42.0	39.1	66.4	63.6
12+	32.3	31.0	46.7	43.8	72.2	71.5
13+	35.0	34.4	49.5	47.7	75.0	77.8
14+	37.0	37.3	51.5	50.6	76.9	82.5

Girls

Girls had weights higher than the respective CDC 2000 z-scores up till 12+ years of age but thereafter, the median and (-2) SD z-scores of weight of girls overlapped with the equivalent CDC 2000 z-scores while the (+2) SD z-scores were lower than the corresponding CDC 2000 z-scores (Figure 4.2.4).

Table 4.2.5 shows that for the median curve at age 6+ years, girls were heavier by 1.4 kg as compared to the CDC 2000 data. The gap increased to 2.9 kg at the age of 11+ and 12+ years. The gap reduced to 1.8 kg at age 13+ years and further reduced to 0.9 kg at 14+ years. At (-2) SD level, girls had weights lower than that of CDC 2000, the difference being 0.3 kg at 14+ years. At (+2) SD level, weights of girls were higher than that of CDC 2000 up to 12+ years. Thereafter weights of girls declined, the difference being 2.8 kg and 5.6 kg lower than the CDC 2000 at 13+ and 14+ years respectively (Table 4.2.5).

WHO 2007 (6-10 years)

Comparison of the weight-for-age z-scores of present study boys and girls with corresponding z-scores of WHO 2007 reference is shown in Figures 4.2.5 and 4.2.6 and Tables 4.2.6 and 4.2.7. The WHO 2007 weight-for-age charts are available only for ages 6-9 years (6.0-9.11 years) and at age 10.0 years so the comparison has been shown for the same.

Boys

The (-2) SD z-scores of boys coincided with that of WHO 2007, median was slightly above and (+2) SD z-scores were way above that of WHO 2007 (Figure 4.2.5). For the median curve at age 6+ years, boys were heavier by 1.4 kg as compared to the WHO 2007 data (Table 4.2.6). The gap increased to 3.5 kg at

10 years. At (-2) SD level, the difference between weights of boys and WHO 2007 was 0.1 kg at age 10 years. For (+2) SD level, the gap progressively increased from 6+ years onwards, the difference being 10.5 kg at age 10 years as compared to the WHO 2007 data (Table 4.2.6).

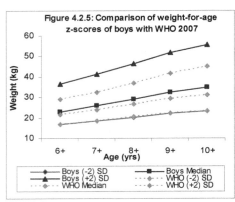

Figure 4.2.5: Comparison of weight-for-age z-scores of boys with WHO 2007

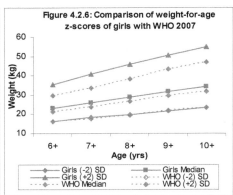

Figure 4.2.6: Comparison of weight-for-age z-scores of girls with WHO 2007

Table 4.2.6: WHO 2007 and present study (PS) weight-for-age (kg) z-scores for boys (n=849)

Age (yrs)	(-2) SD		Median		(+2) SD	
	PS	WHO	PS	WHO	PS	WHO
6+	16.7	16.8	23.1	21.7	36.5	28.9
7+	18.5	18.6	26.0	24.1	41.3	32.6
8+	20.3	20.4	29.2	26.7	46.5	37.0
9+	22.1	22.1	32.4	29.3	51.8	41.7
10+	23.3	23.2	34.7	31.2	55.5	45.0

Table 4.2.7: WHO 2007 and present study (PS) weight-for-age (kg) z-scores for girls (n=848)

Age (yrs)	(-2) SD		Median		(+2) SD	
	PS	WHO	PS	WHO	PS	WHO
6+	16.3	16.0	22.9	21.2	35.5	29.6
7+	18.2	17.6	26.1	23.6	40.8	33.5
8+	19.9	19.6	28.9	26.6	45.7	38.3
9+	21.7	21.8	31.8	29.7	50.7	43.3
10+	23.3	23.3	34.4	31.9	55.1	46.9

Girls

The (-2) SD curve of the present study girls coincided, median was slightly above and the (+2) SD curve was way above that of WHO 2007 (Figure 4.2.6).

For the median curve at age 6+ years, girls were heavier by 1.7 kg as compared to the WHO 2007 data. The gap increased to 2.5 kg at the age of 10 years. At (-2) SD level, there was no difference between weights of girls and WHO 2007; while it was 8.2 kg at (+2) SD level at 10 years respectively (Table 4.2.7).

[B] Prevalence of underweight and overweight using CDC 2000 and WHO 2007

<u>CDC 2000</u>

Age wise percentage prevalence of underweight (< median-2SD of weight-for-age) and overweight (> median+2SD of weight-for-age) in boys and girls is given in Tables 4.2.8 and 4.2.9. Prevalence of underweight was substantially lower, 1.4% and 0.8% in boys and girls respectively. Overweight rates were higher in boys as compared to girls, about 12.2% in boys and 7.5% in girls using CDC 2000.

<u>WHO 2007</u>

Age wise prevalence of underweight (< median-2SD of weight-for-age) and overweight (> median+2SD of weight-for-age) in 6-9 year boys and girls using WHO 2007 is given in Tables 4.2.10 and 4.2.11. Prevalence of underweight was again substantially lower, 1.2% and 0.8% in boys and girls respectively. Overweight rates were higher in boys (19.0%) as compared to girls (13.8%).

Table 4.2.8: Age wise prevalence of normal, underweight and overweight boys using CDC 2000

Age (yrs)	n	< (-2) SD	(-2) to (+2) SD	> (+2) SD
6+	214	5 (2.4)	179 (83.6)	30 (14.0)
7+	200	3 (1.5)	170 (85.0)	27 (13.5)
8+	212	2 (0.9)	180 (84.9)	30 (14.2)
9+	205	1 (0.5)	183 (89.3)	21 (10.2)
10+	201	2 (1.0)	178 (88.6)	21 (10.4)
11+	202	2 (1.0)	172 (85.2)	28 (13.8)
12+	205	3 (1.5)	173 (84.4)	29 (14.1)
13+	245	4 (1.6)	216 (88.2)	25 (10.2)
14+	214	4 (1.9)	188 (87.9)	22 (10.2)
Total	1898	26 (1.4)	1639 (86.4)	233 (12.2)

Figures in parentheses denote percentages

Table 4.2.9: Age wise prevalence of normal, underweight and overweight girls using CDC 2000

Age (yrs)	n	< (-2) SD	(-2) to (+2) SD	> (+2) SD
6+	200	2 (1.0)	172 (86.0)	26 (13.0)
7+	224	4 (1.8)	196 (87.5)	24 (10.7)
8+	202	1 (0.5)	180 (89.1)	21 (10.4)
9+	214	2 (0.9)	203 (94.9)	9 (4.2)
10+	201	2 (1.0)	179 (89.1)	20 (9.9)
11+	202	1 (0.5)	190 (94.1)	11 (5.4)
12+	170	0 (0)	159 (93.5)	11 (6.5)
13+	201	1 (0.5)	195 (97.0)	5 (2.5)
14+	174	2 (1.2)	166 (95.4)	6 (3.4)
Total	1788	15 (0.8)	1640 (91.7)	133 (7.5)

Figures in parentheses denote percentages

Table 4.2.10: Age wise prevalence of normal, underweight and overweight boys using WHO 2007

Age (yrs)	n	< (-2) SD	(-2) to (+2) SD	> (+2) SD
6+	214	5 (2.3)	173 (80.8)	36 (16.9)
7+	200	3 (1.5)	155 (77.5)	42 (21.0)
8+	212	1 (0.5)	171 (80.7)	40 (18.8)
9+	205	1 (0.5)	164 (80.0)	40 (19.5)
Total	831	10 (1.2)	663 (79.8)	158 (19.0)

Figures in parentheses denote percentages

Table 4.2.11: Age wise prevalence of normal, underweight and overweight girls using WHO 2007

Age (yrs)	n	< (-2) SD	(-2) to (+2) SD	> (+2) SD
6+	200	1 (0.5)	168 (84.0)	31 (15.5)
7+	224	3 (1.3)	185 (82.6)	36 (16.1)
8+	202	1 (0.5)	171 (84.7)	30 (14.8)
9+	214	2 (0.9)	193 (90.2)	19 (8.9)
Total	840	7 (0.8)	717 (85.4)	116 (13.8)

Figures in parentheses denote percentages

As expected prevalence rates were higher when WHO 2007 reference was used as compared to CDC 2000 reference.

In present study, using either of the references, the prevalence of overweight was greater in boys as compared to girls. Similar results have been documented from Delhi, Punjab and Chennai (Kaur et al, 2008; Chhatwal et al, 2004; Ramachandran et al, 2002). The subjects in the present study belonged to well-to-do families of professionals, high officials and businessmen who had access to latest technologies and everyday conveniences making them more sedentary. Also, the subjects were not suffering from any dietary constraints that could affect their growth. The sections on dietary pattern and physical activity profile of these subjects will further delineate these findings.

[C] Comparison between CDC 2000 and WHO 2007

Comparison of weight-for-age z-scores by CDC 2000 with WHO 2007 in both boys and girls is given in Figures 4.2.7 and 4.2.8.

The median and the (-2) SD curves of CDC 2000 and WHO 2007 of both boys and girls tracked closely and at most points, there was an overlap, while the (+2) SD curve of CDC 2000 was slightly above that of its WHO 2007 equivalent in both sexes, thus affecting the prevalence of obesity. Since the WHO 2007 weight-for-age charts extend only till 9 years so the comparison has been shown only for ages 6-9 years.

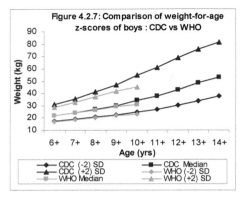
Figure 4.2.7: Comparison of weight-for-age z-scores of boys : CDC vs WHO

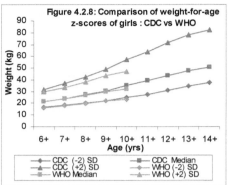
Figure 4.2.8: Comparison of weight-for-age z-scores of girls : CDC vs WHO

The percentage prevalence of normal, underweight and overweight boys and girls using the two references, CDC 2000 and WHO 2007 in 6-9 year old boys, was also compared and is given in Figure 4.2.9. The prevalence rates of overweight (> (+2) SD) were higher using the new WHO 2007 reference compared to CDC 2000 reference (19.0% vs. 13.0% in boys; 13.8% vs. 9.5% in girls). This is because the CDC 2000 growth charts created to update the 1977 NCHS charts, used data from five cross-sectional child growth surveys involving nationally representative samples of populations undergoing increasing trends of overweight and obesity. Thus, the resulting descriptive references are more skewed to the right and underestimate the true rates of overweight and obesity. On the other hand WHO Reference 2007 is a reconstruction of the original 1977 NCHS/WHO reference.

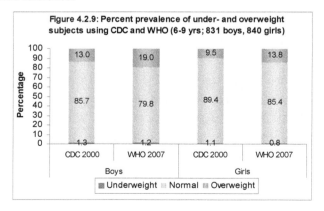
Figure 4.2.9: Percent prevalence of under- and overweight subjects using CDC and WHO (6-9 yrs; 831 boys, 840 girls)

[D] Comparison with Indian upper socioeconomic children

An attempt was made to compare the weight data of the present study with the data from the earlier studies on well-to do Indian children and is presented in Figures 4.2.10 and 4.2.11 and Tables 4.2.12 and 4.2.13. The mean weights reported by the Indian Council of Medical Research (ICMR, 1972; pooled data) on upper socioeconomic children were much lower as compared to the values reported in the present study and by other researchers, both for boys and girls at all ages (Figures 4.2.10 and 4.2.11). This is because ICMR (1972) data were based on measurements of school going children from all over the country (mostly taken from low socio-economic group which formed majority of Indian community).

On comparing the present study data with the mean weights of affluent children reported in the Agarwal et al study, 1992 (India pooled), boys and girls of the present study were heavier than their counterparts were 15 years ago. The median weights of affluent children from Delhi as reported by Agarwal et al (1992) were also much lower than the present study subjects. It is important to mention here, that the statistical method used by Agarwal et al (1992) for smoothening their percentile curves (cubic spline method) was different from that adopted in the present study (LMS method).

The data based on local studies shows that mean weights of Amritsar boys and girls (Prabhjot et al, 2005) were close to those in the present study with a gap of 1 kg at the age of 6+ years which increases to 4 kg in boys and up to 6 kg in girls by 14+ years. However, those from Ernakulum, Kerela (Manuraj et al, 2007) were marginally lower. Mean weights of affluent boys reported by Khanna and Siddhu (2009) were slightly higher than the present study boys; the medians were similar (Table 4.2.12). The mean weights of 9-14 year old Bangalore girls (Sood et al, 2004) were similar to those reported in the present study. A recent study by Marwaha et al (2006) gives weight percentiles for upper socioeconomic children of Delhi (5-17 years) using the LMS method. Comparison showed that boys and girls in the present study were much heavier than the Delhi children studied in 2006 (Tables 4.2.12 and 4.2.13).

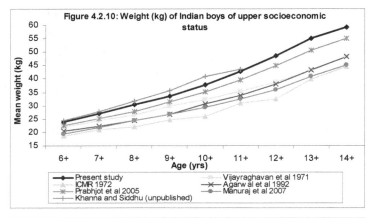

Figure 4.2.10: Weight (kg) of Indian boys of upper socioeconomic status

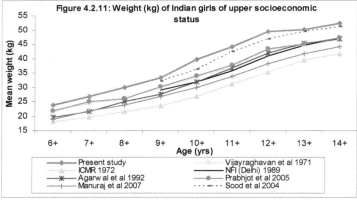

Figure 4.2.11: Weight (kg) of Indian girls of upper socioeconomic status

Figures 4.2.12 and 4.2.13 show comparison of studies done in Delhi over various time periods. There is an upward shift in the weights of boys and girls (10-14 years) indicating nutrition transition and thus a higher predisposition to obesity. These secular changes in growth and development are good indicators of improvements in socioeconomic conditions and in the state of health of the population.

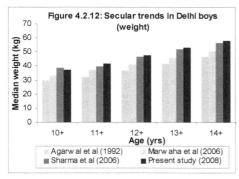
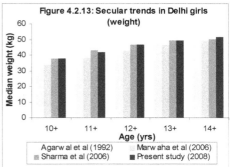

To sum up the findings on weight status of subjects in the present study:

- The median weights of both boys and girls were comparable till the age of 10+ years.
- Between 10-12 years, girls were heavier than boys. After 12+ years, boys continued to gain weight while girls did not.
- In boys, the peak weight gain per year was seen at 13+ years while in girls the peak weight gain per year was seen at 10+ years.
- Weights of both boys and girls in the present study were higher than the CDC 2000 and WHO 2007 references for all the ages.
- Using either of the references, CDC 2000 or WHO 2007, the prevalence of underweight was less than 2% among boys and girls in the present study.
- Prevalence of overweight was higher when WHO 2007 was used as compared to CDC 2000 (19.0% vs. 13.0% in boys; 13.8% vs. 9.5% in girls; 6-9 years).
- Overweight rates were higher in boys as compared to girls.
- Boys and girls in the present study were heavier at all ages compared to earlier studies done on affluent Indian children.
- Comparison of studies done in Delhi over various time periods shows an upward shift in the weights of boys and girls (10-14 years) indicating nutrition transition and thus a higher predisposition to obesity.

Table 4.2.12: Weight (kg) of Indian boys of upper socio-economic status

Place	Author	Year		Age (yrs)								
				6+	7+	8+	9+	10+	11+	12+	13+	14+
India	Vijayraghavan et al	1971	Mean	22.1	24.5	26.4	30.0	32.3	35.3	38.8	42.9	48.3
India	ICMR	1972	Mean	18.7	21.0	22.0	24.7	25.9	31.0	32.5	39.9	44.5
India	Agarwal et al	1992	Mean	20.6	22.4	24.5	26.8	30.8	33.8	37.9	43.2	48.1
Delhi	Agarwal et al	1992	Median	-	-	-	-	29.8	32.4	36.5	41.7	46.6
Delhi	Sharma et al	2006	Median	22.5	25.7	28.7	32.3	38.5	39.9	46.7	52.0	56.7
Delhi	Marwaha et al	2006	Median	21.4	23.8	26.6	29.7	33.1	37.0	41.2	45.9	50.6
Amritsar	Prabhjot et al	2005	Mean	22.6	25.2	27.8	31.4	35.2	39.6	44.8	50.6	55.0
Ernakulum	Manuraj et al	2007	Mean	19.5	21.9	24.5	26.8	29.3	32.6	35.9	40.9	45.1
Delhi	Khanna and Siddhu*	2004-09	Mean	24.3	27.7	31.8	35.7	41.0	43.5	-	-	-
			Median	23.5	26.6	30.6	34.9	39.2	43.4	-	-	-
Present study		2004-09	Median	23.1	26.0	29.2	32.4	37.2	41.6	47.4	53.1	58.2

*PhD Thesis (unpublished)

Table 4.2.13: Weight (kg) of Indian girls of upper socio-economic status

Place	Author	Year		Age (yrs)								
				6+	7+	8+	9+	10+	11+	12+	13+	14+
India	Vijayraghavan et al	1971	Mean	21.6	24.5	26.0	29.8	33.6	37.2	43.0	44.5	46.7
India	ICMR	1972	Mean	18.1	19.7	21.6	23.6	26.7	31.0	35.2	39.3	41.6
India	Agarwal et al	1992	Mean	19.6	21.7	24.9	27.5	31.9	36.8	41.9	45.2	46.6
Delhi	NFI	1989	Mean	-	-	-	28.9	31.9	35.8	40.8	44.6	47.2
Delhi	Agarwal et al	1992	Mean	19.1	20.9	24.7	26.6	32.0	36.9	41.9	46.6	47.6
Delhi	Sharma et al	2006	Median	22.1	24.3	28.7	33.6	37.9	43.2	46.5	49.2	50.3
Delhi	Marwaha et al	2006	Median	21.0	23.5	26.5	29.9	33.9	38.2	42.5	46.3	49.4
Bangalore	Sood et al	2004	Mean	-	-	-	32.1	36.2	42.2	46.7	49.3	51.2
Amritsar	Prabhjot et al	2005	Mean	21.8	25.0	26.0	30.2	34.0	37.6	43.3	45.0	47.1
Ernakulum	Manuraj et al	2007	Mean	18.9	21.8	23.8	26.7	29.9	33.7	38.2	41.5	44.0
Present study		2004-09	Median	22.9	26.1	28.9	31.8	37.6	42.0	46.7	49.5	51.5

4.2.2 Height

The mean height and Δ height per year between 6-14 years for both boys and girls are depicted in Tables 4.2.14 and 4.2.15. Details regarding percentiles of weight for both boys and girls are given in Annexure 8B.

The mean heights of both boys and girls increased with increase in age (Tables 4.2.14 and 4.2.15). There was a progressive increase of 5-6 cm per year up to the age of 9+ years in both boys as well as girls. In subsequent ages, yearly increments in height for boys were 5.0, 5.9, 7.0 and 4.5 cm in 10-11, 11-12, 12-13 and 13-14 years respectively (Table 4.2.14).

In girls, the mean heights significantly increased from 9+ years to 12+ years and thereafter tapered. In other words, increment in height ceased by the age of 13+ years in girls, the peak increase in annual height gain being 8.8 cm at 10+ years which reduced to a marginal increase of 0.8 cm from 13+ to 14+ years (Table 4.2.15). The peak annual increase in height was attained at around the same time as weight (Figure 4.2.1) i.e. 13+ years in boys (7cm/year) as compared to 10+ years in girls (8.8cm/year) (Figure 4.2.14). This is because the adolescent growth spurt occurs earlier in girls (Marshall and Tanner, 1970).

Table 4.2.14 : Height (cm) of boys (n=1898)			
Age (yr)	n	Mean ± SD	Δ height/yr
6+	214	119.9 ± 5.7	-
7+	200	126.2 ± 6.2	6.2
8+	212	131.7 ± 5.6	5.5
9+	205	136.5 ± 6.6	4.8
10+	201	143.1 ± 6.1	6.6
11+	202	148.0 ± 6.4	5.0
12+	205	153.9 ± 7.9	5.9
13+	245	160.9 ± 8.9	7.0
14+	214	165.4 ± 7.9	4.5

Table 4.2.15 : Height (cm) of girls (n=1788)			
Age (yr)	n	Mean ± SD	Δ height/yr
6+	214	119.6 ± 6.0	-
7+	200	125.1 ± 6.2	5.5
8+	212	130.4 ± 6.5	5.3
9+	205	135.4 ± 6.4	5.0
10+	201	144.3 ± 7.3	8.8
11+	202	148.9 ± 7.0	4.6
12+	205	154.2 ± 6.4	5.4
13+	245	156.8 ± 5.6	2.6
14+	214	157.6 ± 5.7	0.8

Tanner (1989) observed peak weight velocity to occur at about the same time as peak height velocity in boys while in girls, peak weight gain lags behind peak height velocity by 6 months. Sood et al (2004) studied height velocity at six monthly intervals and reported that peak weight and height velocity occurred at about the same time among 9-17 year old Bangalore girls.

The height trajectory in Figure 4.2.15 also shows that median heights of both boys and girls were comparable till the age of 9+ years. Girls around 10-12 years of age were slightly taller than boys. However, after the age of 12+ years, median heights in boys continued to increase and were higher than the heights of girls.

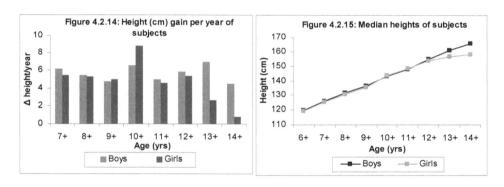

[A] Comparison with international references

Comparison of the height percentiles of boys and girls in the present study was made with two international references; CDC 2000 and WHO 2007.

CDC 2000

The present study data and CDC 2000 reference data for height of boys and girls are compared in Figures 4.2.16 and 4.2.17 and details are given in Tables 4.2.16 and 4.2.17 respectively.

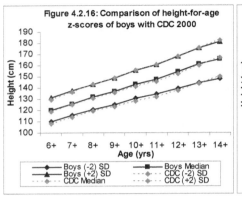

Figure 4.2.16: Comparison of height-for-age z-scores of boys with CDC 2000

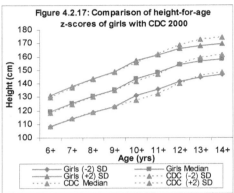

Figure 4.2.17: Comparison of height-for-age z-scores of girls with CDC 2000

Table 4.2.16: CDC 2000 and present study (PS) height-for-age (cm) z-scores for boys (n=1898)

Age (yrs)	(-2) SD		Median		(+2) SD	
	PS	CDC	PS	CDC	PS	CDC
6+	110.2	108.2	119.7	118.6	131.5	129.1
7+	115.7	113.9	125.9	124.9	137.7	136.2
8+	120.6	119.2	131.6	130.8	143.3	143.0
9+	124.8	123.3	136.6	135.7	148.5	148.7
10+	130.4	128.1	143.2	141.5	155.5	155.5
11+	134.2	131.7	147.8	145.7	160.7	160.5
12+	139.4	137.4	154.5	152.4	168.4	168.1
13+	144.4	143.9	161.0	160.0	175.9	175.9
14+	147.9	150.2	165.8	167.0	181.3	182.2

Table 4.2.17: CDC 2000 and present study (PS) height-for-age (cm) z-scores for girls (n=1788)

Age (yrs)	(-2) SD		Median		(+2) SD	
	PS	CDC	PS	CDC	PS	CDC
6+	108.5	108.1	119.2	118.2	131.0	129.5
7+	114.0	113.8	125.4	124.6	137.9	136.7
8+	118.6	118.8	130.4	130.3	143.4	143.0
9+	123.1	122.7	135.3	135.0	148.8	148.3
10+	131.0	127.6	143.6	141.3	157.3	155.8
11+	135.7	132.1	148.3	146.9	161.5	161.7
12+	141.7	139.9	153.8	154.5	166.1	168.6
13+	144.8	145.6	156.6	159.1	168.3	172.5
14+	146.6	148.1	158.1	161.1	169.4	174.3

Boys

There was a progressive increase in heights of boys up till 14+ years of age (Figure 4.2.16). The height trajectory of both boys and girls followed similar path as the CDC 2000 reference. The median, (-2) and (+2) SD curves of boys in the present study and the corresponding CDC 2000 curves, tracked very closely and at most age points there was an overlap.

Table 4.2.16 shows that for the median curve, boys had heights similar to the CDC 2000 up till 9+ years of age, the difference being more distinct from 10-13 years of age. At age 6+ years, boys were taller by 1.1 cm as compared to the CDC 2000 data. They were shorter by 1.2 cm at the age of 14+ years.

At (-2) and (+2) SD level, boys had heights lower than that of CDC 2000, the difference being 2.3 cm and 0.9 cm, respectively at age 14+ years (Table 4.2.16).

Girls

The median, (-2) SD and (+2) SD z-scores of girls for heights were comparable to the CDC 2000 up till 9+ years of age, higher than CDC between 10-11 years after which they were lower than the equivalent CDC 2000 z-scores (Figure 4.2.17).

For the median curve, the girls in the present study had heights similar to the CDC 2000 up till 9+ years of age. At age 6+ years, girls in the present study were taller by 1.0 cm as compared to the CDC 2000 data (Table 4.2.17). The gap increased to 2.3 cm and 1.4 cm at the age of 10+ and 11+ years respectively after which girls in the present study had heights lower than the CDC 2000, the difference being 2.5 cm and 3.0 cm at 13+ and 14+ years respectively. At (-2) SD level, the difference between CDC 2000 and heights of girls was 1.5 cm, which was 4.9 cm at (+2) SD level at 14+ years respectively.

WHO 2007

The present study data and WHO 2007 reference data for height of boys and girls are compared in Figures 4.2.18 and 4.2.19 and details are given in Tables 4.2.18 and 4.2.19 respectively.

Boys

The median, (-2) and (+2) SD curves of boys and the WHO 2007 reference, tracked closely and at some age points there was an overlap (Figure 4.2.18).

For the median curve, the boys in the present study had heights similar to the WHO 2007 up till 9+ years of age, the difference being more distinct from 10-13 years of age. At age 6+ years, boys in the present study were taller by 0.8 cm as compared to the WHO 2007 data, the difference reduced to zero at the age of 14+ years (Table 4.2.18).

At (-2) SD level, boys in the present study had heights higher than that of WHO 2007 for all ages except at age 14+, the difference being 2.4 cm. The (+2) SD of boys in the present study was higher than that of WHO 2007 for all ages (Table 4.2.18).

Girls

The median, (-2) SD and (+2) SD z-scores of girls for heights were comparable to WHO 2007 up to the age of 12+ years, after which they were lower than the equivalent WHO z-scores (Figure 4.2.19).

Table 4.2.19 shows that for the median curve, at age 6+ years, girls in the present study were taller by 1.2 cm as compared to the WHO 2007 data. The gap was 1.3 cm and reduced to 0.6 cm at the age of 10+ and 11+ years respectively, after which girls had heights lower than the WHO 2007, the difference being 1.7 cm and 2.6 cm at 13+ and 14+ years respectively. At (-2) SD level, the difference between WHO 2007 and heights of girls was 0.3 cm, which was 5.2 cm at (+2) SD level at 14+ years respectively (Table 4.2.19).

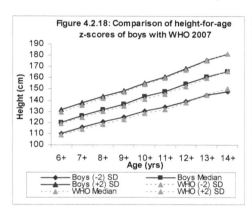

Figure 4.2.18: Comparison of height-for-age z-scores of boys with WHO 2007

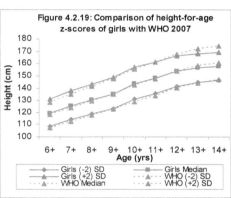

Figure 4.2.19: Comparison of height-for-age z-scores of girls with WHO 2007

Table 4.2.18: WHO 2007 and present study (PS) height-for-age (cm) z-scores for boys (n=1898)

Age (yrs)	(-2) SD		Median		(+2) SD	
	PS	WHO	PS	WHO	PS	WHO
6+	110.2	108.7	119.7	118.9	131.5	129.1
7+	115.7	113.6	125.9	124.5	137.7	135.5
8+	120.6	118.3	131.6	129.9	143.3	141.6
9+	124.8	122.4	136.6	134.7	148.5	147.1
10+	130.4	127.7	143.2	140.8	155.5	154.0
11+	134.2	131.7	147.8	145.5	160.7	159.3
12+	139.4	137.9	154.5	152.4	168.4	167.0
13+	144.4	144.5	161.0	159.7	175.9	174.8
14+	147.9	150.3	165.8	165.8	181.3	181.3

Table 4.2.19: WHO 2007 and present study (PS) height-for-age (cm) z-scores for girls (n=1788)

Age (yrs)	(-2) SD		Median		(+2) SD	
	PS	WHO	PS	WHO	PS	WHO
6+	108.5	107.4	119.2	118.0	131.0	128.6
7+	114.0	112.4	125.4	123.7	137.9	134.9
8+	118.6	117.6	130.4	129.5	143.4	141.4
9+	123.1	122.6	135.3	135.0	148.8	147.5
10+	131.0	129.2	143.6	142.3	157.3	155.4
11+	135.7	134.2	148.3	147.7	161.5	161.1
12+	141.7	140.2	153.8	154.0	166.1	167.8
13+	144.8	144.4	156.6	158.3	168.3	172.2
14+	146.6	146.9	158.1	160.7	169.4	174.6

[B] Prevalence of stunting using CDC 2000 and WHO 2007

CDC 2000

Age wise prevalence of stunting (< median-2SD of height-for-age) is given in Table 4.2.20 and 4.2.21. Percentage of stunting was low (1.2%) in boys. Stunting rates in girls was also low, about 2.1%. These subjects belonged to well-to-do sections of the society and were not suffering from any dietary constraints which could have an affect on the expression of genetic potential for growth.

Table 4.2.20: Age wise prevalence of stunting in boys using CDC 2000

Age (yrs)	n	< (-2) SD	(-2) to (+2) SD	> (+2) SD
6+	214	1 (0.5)	202 (94.4)	11 (5.1)
7+	200	0 (0)	185 (92.5)	15 (7.5)
8+	212	2 (0.9)	206 (97.2)	4 (1.9)
9+	205	5 (2.4)	195 (95.2)	5 (2.4)
10+	201	2 (1.0)	196 (97.5)	3 (1.5)
11+	202	0 (0)	199 (98.5)	3 (1.5)
12+	205	2 (1.0)	198 (96.6)	5 (2.4)
13+	245	4 (1.6)	234 (95.5)	7 (2.9)
14+	214	7 (3.3)	206 (96.3)	1 (0.4)
Total	1898	23 (1.2)	1821 (95.9)	54 (2.9)

Figures in parentheses denote percentages

Table 4.2.21: Age wise prevalence of stunting in girls using CDC 2000

Age (yrs)	n	< (-2) SD	(-2) to (+2) SD	> (+2) SD
6+	200	3 (1.5)	187 (93.5)	10 (5.0)
7+	224	7 (3.1)	208 (92.9)	9 (4.0)
8+	202	5 (2.5)	192 (95.0)	5 (2.5)
9+	214	5 (2.3)	205 (95.8)	4 (1.9)
10+	201	2 (1.0)	187 (93.0)	12 (6.0)
11+	202	2 (1.0)	196 (97.0)	4 (2.0)
12+	170	1 (0.6)	165 (97.1)	4 (2.3)
13+	201	4 (2.0)	197 (98.0)	0 (0)
14+	174	8 (4.6)	166 (95.4)	0 (0)
Total	1788	37 (2.1)	1703 (95.2)	48 (2.7)

Figures in parentheses denote percentages

WHO 2007

Age wise prevalence of stunting (< median-2SD of height-for-age) is given in Tables 4.2.22 and 4.2.23. Percentage of stunting was low in boys as well as in girls (1.3% and 1.7%). In case of girls, the CDC 2000 reference reflected a somewhat shorter sample than the WHO 2007 (2.1% vs. 1.7%).

Table 4.2.22: Age wise prevalence of stunting in boys using WHO 2007

Age (yrs)	n	< (-2) SD	(-2) to (+2) SD	> (+2) SD
6+	214	1 (0.5)	202 (94.4)	11 (5.1)
7+	200	0 (0)	185 (92.5)	15 (7.5)
8+	212	2 (0.9)	206 (97.2)	4 (1.9)
9+	205	4 (2.0)	193 (94.1)	8 (3.9)
10+	201	2 (1.0)	192 (95.5)	7 (3.5)
11+	202	0 (0)	196 (97.0)	6 (3.0)
12+	205	4 (2.0)	195 (95.1)	6 (2.9)
13+	245	5 (2.0)	232 (94.7)	8 (3.3)
14+	214	7 (3.3)	203 (94.9)	4 (1.9)
Total	1898	25 (1.3)	1804 (95.0)	69 (3.7)

Figures in parentheses denote percentages

Table 4.2.23: Age wise prevalence of stunting in girls using WHO 2007

Age (yrs)	n	< (-2) SD	(-2) to (+2) SD	> (+2) SD
6+	200	2 (1.0)	186 (93.0)	12 (6.0)
7+	224	3 (1.3)	209 (93.3)	12 (5.4)
8+	202	2 (1.0)	193 (95.5)	7 (3.5)
9+	214	6 (2.8)	203 (94.9)	5 (2.3)
10+	201	3 (1.6)	185 (92.0)	13 (6.4)
11+	202	4 (2.0)	193 (95.5)	5 (2.5)
12+	170	2 (1.2)	164 (96.5)	4 (2.3)
13+	201	3 (1.6)	198 (98.5)	0 (0)
14+	174	6 (3.5)	168 (96.5)	0 (0)
Total	1788	31 (1.7)	1699 (95.0)	58 (3.3)

Figures in parentheses denote percentages

[C] Comparison between CDC 2000 and WHO 2007

Comparison of height-for-age z-scores by CDC 2000 with WHO 2007 in both boys and girls are given in Figures 4.2.20 and 4.2.21. The (-2) SD and the median z-scores of CDC 2000 of both boys and girls coincided with equivalent

WHO 2007 z-scores, while the (+2) SD z-scores of CDC 2000 were slightly above that of WHO 2007.

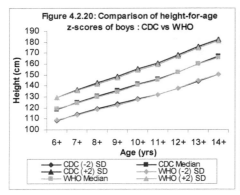
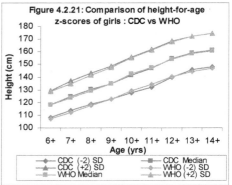

The percentage prevalence of stunting in boys and girls using the two references, CDC 2000 and WHO 2007, was also compared and is given in Figure 4.2.22. The prevalence rates of stunting (< (-2) SD) were similar in boys using either of the references. In girls stunting rates were slightly higher using the CDC 2000 reference as compared to the WHO 2007 reference.

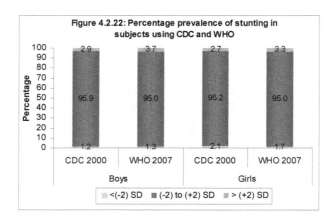

[D] Comparison with Indian upper socioeconomic children

An attempt was made to compare the height data of the present study with the data from the earlier studies on well-to do Indian children and is presented in Figures 4.2.23 and 4.2.24 and Tables 4.2.24 and 4.2.25. The mean heights reported by ICMR (1972, pooled data) on upper socioeconomic children were much lower as compared to the values reported in the present study and by other investigators, both for boys and girls at all ages.

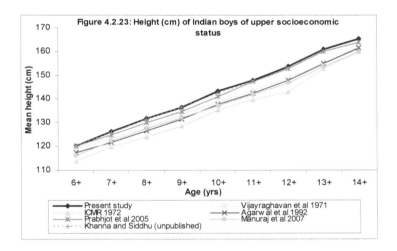

Figure 4.2.23: Height (cm) of Indian boys of upper socioeconomic status

On comparing the present study data with the mean heights of affluent children reported in the Agarwal et al study, 1992 (India pooled), boys and girls of the present study were taller than their counterparts were 15 years ago.

The data based on local studies shows that mean heights of Amritsar boys and girls (Prabhjot et al 2005) were close to those in the present study with a gap of 2 cm in boys and 1.9 cm in girls at the age of 14+ years. However, those from Ernakulum, Kerela (Manuraj et al 2007) were shorter than present study subjects. The mean heights of 6-11 year old boys reported by Khanna and

Siddhu (2009) were exactly similar to that of boys in the present study. Also, the mean heights of 9-14 year Bangalore girls (Sood et al, 2004) were close to those reported for girls in the present study. A recent study by Marwaha et al (2006) gives height percentiles for upper socioeconomic children of Delhi (5-17 years) using the LMS method. Comparison showed that boys and girls in the present study were much taller than the Delhi children studied by Marwaha et al in 2006 (Table 4.2b.13 and 4.2b.14).

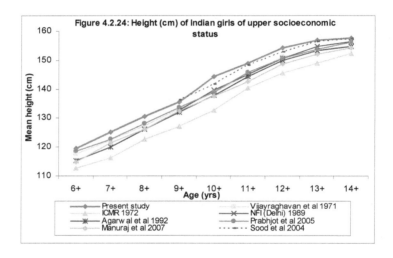

Figures 4.2.25 and 4.2.26 show comparison of studies done in Delhi over various time periods. There was an upward shift in the heights of boys and girls (10-14 years) indicating nutrition transition. These secular changes in growth and development could be attributed to better environment and nutrition of these subjects.

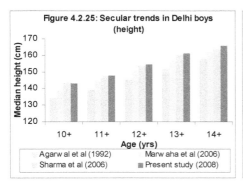

Figure 4.2.25: Secular trends in Delhi boys (height)

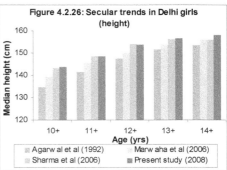

Figure 4.2.26: Secular trends in Delhi girls (height)

To sum up the findings on height status of subjects in the present study:

- The median heights of both boys and girls were comparable till the age of 9+ years.
- In girls, the median heights increased from 9+ years to 12+ years and thereafter tapered. After the age of 12+ years, median heights in boys continued to increase and were higher than the heights of girls.
- The peak annual increase in height was attained around 13+ years in boys (7cm/year) as compared to 10+ years in girls (8.8cm/year).
- Height-for-age z-scores of boys were comparable to the CDC 2000 and WHO 2007 references for all the ages. Girls had heights comparable to the CDC 2000 and WHO 2007 references up to the age of 12+ years, after which they were lower than the equivalent CDC 2000 and WHO z-scores.
- Using either of the references, CDC 2000 or WHO 2007, the prevalence of stunting was not more than 2% among boys and girls in the present study.
- Boys and girls in the present study were taller at all ages compared to earlier studies done on affluent Indian children.
- Comparison of studies done in Delhi over various time periods showed an upward shift in the heights of boys and girls (10-14 years) indicating nutrition transition.

Table 4.2.24: Heights (cm) of Indian boys of upper socio-economic status

Place	Author	Year		Age (yrs)								
				6+	7+	8+	9+	10+	11+	12+	13+	14+
India	Vijayraghavan et al	1971	Mean	118.9	123.3	127.7	133.6	138.5	143.5	148.9	154.9	161.7
India	ICMR	1972	Mean	113.8	119.7	123.9	128.4	135.4	139.6	142.8	152.9	159.9
India	Agarwal et al	1992	Mean	117.5	121.6	126.4	131.5	137.6	142.3	147.9	154.9	161.4
Delhi	Agarwal et al	1992	Median	-	-	-	-	134.2	139.1	145.1	151.5	158.0
Amritsar	Prabhjot et al	2005	Mean	120.0	124.8	130.0	134.8	141.0	147.4	152.9	159.9	163.8
Delhi	Sharma et al	2006	Median	119.5	125.0	130.5	137.7	143.4	147.5	153.6	160.3	163.7
Delhi	Marwaha et al	2006	Median	118.5	123.3	128.3	133.4	138.8	144.5	150.5	156.5	162.0
Ernakulum	Manuraj et al	2007	Mean	116.1	122.0	127.4	132.1	137.1	141.9	146.7	153.7	159.8
Delhi	Khanna and Siddhu*	2004-09	Mean	120.1	125.5	131.5	136.6	142.3	147.4	-	-	-
			Median	119.5	125.5	131.4	136.8	142.4	148.3	-	-	-
Present study		2004-09	Median	119.7	125.9	131.6	136.6	143.2	147.8	154.5	161.0	165.8

*PhD Thesis (unpublished)

Table 4.2.25: Heights (cm) of Indian girls of upper socio-economic status

Place	Author	Year		Age (yrs)								
				6+	7+	8+	9+	10+	11+	12+	13+	14+
India	Vijayraghavan et al	1971	Mean	117.7	122.6	127.2	133.1	138.9	145.0	151.0	153.4	155.0
India	ICMR	1972	Mean	112.6	116.3	122.8	127.1	132.5	140.6	145.5	149.0	152.4
Delhi	NFI	1989	Mean	-	-	-	132.7	139.7	145.0	150.6	154.8	156.4
India	Agarwal et al	1992	Mean	115.4	120.2	126.2	131.9	137.9	144.3	149.9	153.2	154.8
Delhi	Agarwal et al	1992	Median	-	-	-	127.7	134.7	141.6	147.5	151.5	153.5
Bangalore	Sood et al	2004	Mean	-	-	-	136.2	141.7	148.3	152.9	156.3	157.4
Amritsar	Prabhjot et al	2005	Mean	118.7	122.8	128.1	133.6	139.0	145.9	150.6	153.7	156.2
Delhi	Sharma et al	2006	Median	119.8	123.7	129.8	135.6	143.1	149.5	154	156.4	155.8
Delhi	Marwaha et al	2006	Median	116.5	121.9	127.5	133.4	139.4	145.2	150.1	153.7	156.0
Ernakulum	Manuraj et al	2007	Mean	114.8	121.6	126.2	132.3	137.6	142.8	148.6	152.1	154.2
Present study		2004-09	Median	119.2	125.4	130.4	135.3	143.6	148.3	153.8	156.6	158.1

4.2.3 BMI

The mean BMI and ΔBMI per year between 6-14 years for both boys and girls are depicted in Tables 4.2.26 and 4.2.27. Details regarding percentiles of BMI for both boys and girls are given in Annexure 8C.

BMI increased with increase in age in both boys and girls (Tables 4.2.26 and 4.2.27). There was a steady increase of 0.3-0.5 kg/m^2 per year up to the age of 9+ years in both boys as well as girls. Thereafter, BMI of girls rose higher than that of boys up till 12+ years. The peak increase in annual BMI gain (1.2 kg/m^2 per year) was seen at 10+ years in girls and it continued to remain high till 12+ years, after which BMI declined (Figure 4.2.27). In boys, a gradual increase in mean BMI was seen from 11+ years and it continued to remain high till 14+ years. The peak annual increase in BMI (1.4 kg/m^2 per year) was seen at 11+ years in boys (Figure 4.2.27).

Table 4.2.26 : BMI (kg/m^2) of boys (n=1898)			
Age (yr)	n	Mean ± SD	Δ BMI/yr
6+	214	16.4 ± 2.6	-
7+	200	16.9 ± 2.8	0.5
8+	212	17.4 ± 3.2	0.5
9+	205	17.9 ± 2.9	0.5
10+	201	18.4 ± 3.5	0.5
11+	202	19.8 ± 3.9	1.4
12+	205	20.3 ± 4.5	0.5
13+	245	21.1 ± 4.0	0.8
14+	214	21.7 ± 4.3	0.6

Table 4.2.27 : BMI (kg/m^2) of girls (n=1788)			
Age (yr)	n	Mean ± SD	Δ BMI/yr
6+	200	16.6 ± 2.5	-
7+	224	16.9 ± 2.7	0.3
8+	202	17.4 ± 2.8	0.5
9+	214	17.7 ± 2.9	0.3
10+	201	18.9 ± 3.9	1.2
11+	202	19.9 ± 3.5	1.0
12+	170	20.7 ± 3.6	0.8
13+	201	20.4 ± 3.6	-0.3
14+	174	21.1 ± 3.8	0.7

The BMI trajectory in Figure 4.2.28 also shows that the median BMI of girls was slightly higher than that of boys till 8+ years. The two curves track closely and crossover at age 12+ years, so that by age 14+, median BMI of boys was 0.8 kg/m^2 higher as compared to BMI of girls.

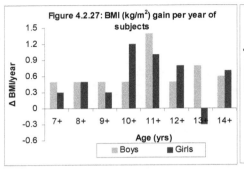
Figure 4.2.27: BMI (kg/m^2) gain per year of subjects

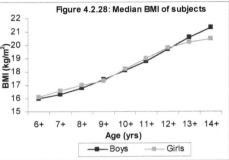
Figure 4.2.28: Median BMI of subjects

[A] Comparison with international references

Comparison of the BMI-for-age z-scores of boys and girls in the present study was made with two international references i.e. *CDC 2000* and *WHO 2007*. Prevalence of under-nutrition and over-nutrition was then estimated.

CDC 2000

The present study data and CDC 2000 reference data for BMI of boys and girls are compared in Figures 4.2.29 and 4.2.30 and details are given in Tables 4.2.28 and 4.2.29.

Boys

The median and (+2) SD z-scores of BMI of boys in the present study were higher than the respective CDC 2000 z-scores for all ages while the (-2) SD curve of boys was lower than its CDC 2000 equivalent (Figure 4.2.29).

Table 4.2.28 shows that for the median curve, the boys in the present study had higher BMI than the CDC 2000 for all the ages, the difference being more distinct from 10+ years of age. At age 6+ years, BMI of boys in the present study was 0.6

kg/m^2 higher as compared to the CDC 2000 data. The gap increased to 1.9 kg/m^2 at 14+ years.

At (-2) SD level, boys had lower BMI than that of CDC 2000, the difference being 0.9 kg/m^2 at 14+ years. For (+2) SD curve at age 14+ years, BMI values of present study boys were higher, the difference being 3.4 kg/m^2 as compared to the equivalent CDC 2000 z-scores (Table 4.2.28).

Girls

The present study girls had median BMI higher than the CDC 2000 for all ages (Figure 4.2.30). For the median curve at age 6+ years, BMI of girls was higher by 0.8 kg/m^2 as compared to the CDC 2000 data (Table 4.2.29). The gap increased to 1.4 kg/m^2 at the age of 11+ and 12+ years and finally reduced back to 0.9 kg/m^2 at age 14+ years.

For the (-2) SD curve, girls presented a similar pattern to those observed for boys up till 11+ years, after which the values overlap. For the (+2) SD curve, the largest disparity was seen at 6+ years, where the BMI curve of girls was 1.7 kg/m^2 above the CDC 2000 z-score value. But the differences reduced to negligible by 14+ years (Table 4.2.29).

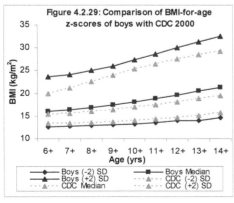

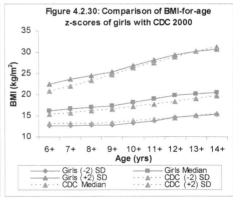

Table 4.2.28: CDC 2000 and present study (PS) BMI-for-age (kg/m^2) z-scores for boys (n=1898)

Age (yrs)	(-2) SD		Median		(+2) SD	
	PS	CDC	PS	CDC	PS	CDC
6+	12.7	13.4	16.0	15.4	23.6	20.0
7+	12.8	13.4	16.3	15.6	24.2	21.2
8+	12.9	13.5	16.8	16.0	25.1	22.6
9+	13.1	13.7	17.4	16.4	26.0	23.9
10+	13.3	14.0	18.1	17.0	27.4	25.4
11+	13.5	14.3	18.8	17.5	28.6	26.4
12+	14.0	14.7	19.7	18.1	30.0	27.6
13+	14.1	15.2	20.6	18.8	31.3	28.5
14+	14.7	15.7	21.3	19.4	32.5	29.3

Table 4.2.29: CDC 2000 and present study (PS) BMI-for-age (kg/m^2) z-scores for girls (n=1788)

Age (yrs)	(-2) SD		Median		(+2) SD	
	PS	CDC	PS	CDC	PS	CDC
6+	12.6	13.1	16.1	15.3	22.5	20.8
7+	12.7	13.1	16.6	15.6	23.6	22.0
8+	12.8	13.2	17.0	16.1	24.5	23.4
9+	12.8	13.4	17.3	16.5	25.3	24.7
10+	13.4	13.8	18.2	17.2	26.9	26.3
11+	13.9	14.1	19.0	17.7	28.2	27.5
12+	14.6	14.5	19.8	18.4	29.4	28.9
13+	15.0	15.0	20.2	19.0	30.1	30.1
14+	15.4	15.5	20.5	19.6	30.7	31.1

WHO 2007

On applying the WHO 2007 z-scores, both boys and girls presented similar patterns to those observed using CDC 2000 z-scores with an exception that the differences in the WHO 2007 (+2) SD z scores was larger than the corresponding differences in the CDC 2000 z-scores.

Boys

The median and (+2) SD curves of BMI of boys in the present study were higher than the respective WHO 2007 z-scores for all ages while the (-2) SD curve of boys was lower than its WHO 2007 equivalent (Figure 4.2.31).

For the median curve, the boys in the present study had BMI higher than the WHO 2007 for all the ages, the difference being more evident from 10+ years of age. At age 6+ years, BMI of boys in the present study was 0.6 kg/m² higher as compared to the WHO 2007 data. The gap increased to 2.0 kg/m² at 14+ years (Table 4.2.30). At (-2) SD level, boys had BMI slightly lower than that of WHO 2007, the difference being 1.0 kg/m² at 14+ years. For (+2) SD curve at age 14+ years, BMI values of boys in the present study were substantially higher, the difference being 6.1 kg/m² as compared to the equivalent WHO z-scores. The difference was nearly half (3.4 kg/m²) when equivalent CDC 2000 z-scores were used (Table 4.2.30).

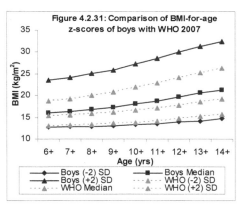

Figure 4.2.31: Comparison of BMI-for-age z-scores of boys with WHO 2007

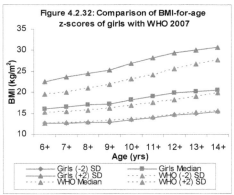

Figure 4.2.32: Comparison of BMI-for-age z-scores of girls with WHO 2007

Table 4.2.30: WHO 2007 and present study (PS) BMI-for-age (kg/m²) z-scores for boys (n=1898)

Age (yrs)	(-2) SD		Median		(+2) SD	
	PS	WHO	PS	WHO	PS	WHO
6+	12.7	13.1	16.0	15.4	23.6	18.7
7+	12.8	13.2	16.3	15.6	24.2	19.3
8+	12.9	13.4	16.8	15.9	25.1	20.1
9+	13.1	13.6	17.4	16.2	26.0	20.8
10+	13.3	13.9	18.1	16.7	27.4	22.0
11+	13.5	14.2	18.8	17.1	28.6	22.9
12+	14.0	14.7	19.7	17.8	30.0	24.2
13+	14.1	15.2	20.6	18.6	31.3	25.3
14+	14.7	15.7	21.3	19.3	32.5	26.4

Table 4.2.31: WHO 2007 and present study (PS) BMI-for-age (kg/m^2) z-scores for girls (n=1788)

Age (yrs)	(-2) SD		Median		(+2) SD	
	PS	WHO	PS	WHO	PS	WHO
6+	12.6	12.7	16.1	15.3	22.5	19.5
7+	12.7	12.8	16.6	15.5	23.6	20.1
8+	12.8	13.0	17.0	15.8	24.5	21.0
9+	12.8	13.3	17.3	16.3	25.3	21.9
10+	13.4	13.7	18.2	16.9	26.9	23.2
11+	13.9	14.1	19.0	17.5	28.2	24.2
12+	14.6	14.7	19.8	18.3	29.4	25.6
13+	15.0	15.2	20.2	19.1	30.1	26.8
14+	15.4	15.6	20.5	19.8	30.7	27.7

Girls

The patterns observed in the boys' curves were also evident among girls (Figure 4.2.32), except that the differences in the median and (+2) SD curves were smaller in girls than the corresponding differences in the boys' z-scores.

The present study girls had median BMI higher than the CDC for all ages. For the median curve at age 6+ years, BMI of girls was higher by 0.8 kg/m^2 as compared to the CDC data. The gap increased to 1.4 kg/m^2 at the age of 11+ and 12+ years and finally reduced to 0.6 kg/m^2 at age 14+ years (Table 4.2.31). The (-2) SD curve of girls tracked closely to the corresponding WHO (-2) SD curve up till 10+ years, after which the values overlapped. The (+2) SD curve was way above that of WHO, the difference being 3 kg/m^2 at 6+ and 14+ years respectively.

[B] Prevalence of under-nutrition and over-nutrition

CDC 2000

Age wise prevalence of under-nutrition (< median-2SD of BMI-for-age) and over-nutrition (> median+2SD of BMI-for-age) is given in Tables 4.2.32 and 4.2.33. Prevalence of under-nutrition was low among both boys and girls, 3.0% and

1.3% respectively. Over-nutrition rates were higher among boys (16.2%) as compared to girls (9.3%).

Table 4.2.32: Age wise prevalence of under- and over-nutrition in boys using CDC 2000

Age (yrs)	n	< (-2) SD	(-2) to (+2) SD	> (+2) SD
6+	214	11 (5.1)	164 (76.6)	39 (18.2)
7+	200	6 (3.0)	156 (78.0)	38 (19.0)
8+	212	7 (3.3)	170 (80.2)	35 (16.5)
9+	205	3 (1.5)	176 (85.9)	26 (12.6)
10+	201	8 (4.0)	166 (82.6)	27 (13.4)
11+	202	5 (2.5)	154 (76.2)	43 (21.3)
12+	205	6 (2.9)	162 (79.0)	37 (18.0)
13+	245	5 (2.0)	205 (83.7)	35 (14.3)
14+	214	6 (2.8)	181 (84.6)	27 (12.6)
Total	1898	57 (3.0)	1534 (80.8)	307 (16.2)

Figures in parentheses denote percentages

Table 4.2.33: Age wise prevalence of under- and over-nutrition in girls using CDC 2000

Age (yrs)	n	< (-2) SD	(-2) to (+2) SD	> (+2) SD
6+	200	2 (1.0)	171 (85.5)	27 (13.5)
7+	224	6 (2.7)	194 (86.6)	24 (10.7)
8+	202	2 (1.0)	179 (88.6)	21 (9.4)
9+	214	3 (1.4)	196 (91.6)	15 (7.0)
10+	201	7 (3.5)	175 (87.1)	19 (9.4)
11+	202	2 (1.0)	181 (89.6)	19 (9.4)
12+	170	0 (0)	150 (88.2)	20 (11.8)
13+	201	1 (0.5)	189 (94.0)	11 (5.5)
14+	174	1 (0.6)	163 (93.7)	10 (5.7)
Total	1788	24 (1.3)	1598 (89.4)	166 (9.3)

Figures in parentheses denote percentages

WHO 2007

Tables 4.2.34 and 4.2.35 give the age wise prevalence of under-nutrition (< median-2SD of BMI-for-age) and over-nutrition (> median+2SD of BMI-for-age) in boys and girls using WHO 2007 reference. Under-nutrition rates using WHO 2007 were similar to those estimated using CDC 2000 reference in both boys (3.0%) and girls (1.4% and 1.3%) while over-nutrition rates were higher using

WHO 2007. Prevalence of over-nutrition was higher in boys (23.8%) as compared to girls (13.8%).

Table 4.2.34: Age wise prevalence of under- and over-nutrition in boys using WHO 2007

Age (yrs)	n	< (-2) SD	(-2) to (+2) SD	> (+2) SD
6+	214	8 (3.7)	158 (73.8)	48 (22.4)
7+	200	4 (2.0)	150 (75.0)	46 (23.0)
8+	212	6 (2.8)	158 (74.5)	48 (22.6)
9+	205	3 (1.5)	155 (75.6)	47 (22.9)
10+	201	9 (4.5)	143 (71.1)	49 (24.4)
11+	202	5 (2.5)	134 (66.3)	63 (31.2)
12+	205	6 (3.0)	145 (70.7)	54 (26.3)
13+	245	7 (2.9)	182 (74.3)	56 (22.8)
14+	214	8 (3.8)	164 (76.6)	42 (19.6)
Total	**1898**	**56 (3.0)**	**1389 (73.2)**	**453 (23.8)**

Figures in parentheses denote percentages

Table 4.2.35: Age wise prevalence of under- and over-nutrition in girls using WHO 2007

Age (yrs)	n	< (-2) SD	(-2) to (+2) SD	> (+2) SD
6+	200	0 (0)	170 (85.0)	30 (15.0)
7+	224	4 (1.8)	184 (82.1)	36 (16.1)
8+	202	1 (0.5)	170 (84.2)	31 (15.3)
9+	214	3 (1.4)	179 (83.6)	32 (15.0)
10+	201	8 (4.0)	167 (83.1)	26 (12.9)
11+	202	3 (1.5)	167 (82.7)	32 (15.8)
12+	170	2 (1.2)	142 (83.5)	26 (15.3)
13+	201	3 (1.5)	180 (89.6)	18 (8.9)
14+	174	1 (0.6)	157 (90.2)	16 (9.2)
Total	**1788**	**25 (1.4)**	**1516 (84.8)**	**247 (13.8)**

Figures in parentheses denote percentages

[C] Comparison between CDC 2000 and WHO 2007

Figures 4.2.33 and 4.2.34 show the comparison of BMI-for-age z-scores of WHO 2007 with CDC 2000. The (-2) SD and the median curves of CDC and WHO of both boys and girls tracked closely and at most age points, there was an overlap, while the (+2) SD curve of CDC was way above that of its WHO 2007 equivalent in both sexes, thus affecting the prevalence of obesity.

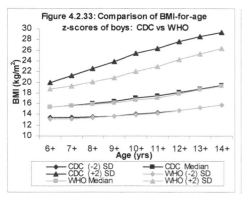
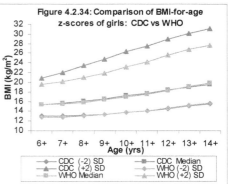

The percentage prevalence of normal, under- and over-nourished boys and girls using the two references, CDC 2000 and WHO 2007 was also compared and is given in Figure 4.2.35. The prevalence rates of over-nutrition were higher using the WHO 2007 reference as compared to the CDC 2000 reference. This is because the CDC 2000 growth charts created to update the 1977 NCHS charts, used data from five cross-sectional child growth surveys involving nationally representative samples of populations undergoing increasing trends of overweight and obesity. Thus, the resulting descriptive references are more skewed to the right and underestimate the true rates of over-nutrition. On the other hand WHO Reference 2007 is a reconstruction of the original 1977 NCHS/WHO.

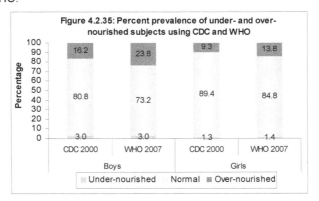

The use of WHO 2007 reference is thus recommended over CDC 2000 reference. Since the (-2) SD curve of WHO 2007 and CDC 2000 overlap, the under-nutrition rates were similar using either CDC 2000 or WHO 2007 z-scores.

In both boys and girls, high over-nutrition rates were present as early as 6 years. About 22.4 % boys and 15% girls studying in class I were over-nourished using the WHO 2007 criteria. High BMI in preschool children has been reported in other studies as well (Marwaha et al 2006, Sharma et al, 2006). The anthropometric data suggests that any intervention planned to combat the menace of over-nutrition in childhood should begin very early in life.

Over-nutrition rates among girls were high beginning from 6+ years and remained high during the pubertal age group as was seen in other studies in Chennai (Ramachandran et al, 2002), Bangalore (Sood et al, 2004) and Delhi (Kaur et al, 2008) and perhaps because of increased adipose tissue and overall body weight of girls during puberty. The prevalence of over-nutrition was marginally less in the post pubertal period. It has been reported earlier that the number of fat cells increase during periods of rapid growth, thereafter increased fat typically accumulates by increasing size of fat cells already present (Laxmaiah et al, 2007). Among boys over-nutrition rates were high during the prepubertal years by either reference and decreased as age advanced.

In the present study, using either of the references, WHO 2007 or CDC 2000, over-nutrition rates were higher in boys as compared to girls. Similar results have been documented from Delhi, Punjab and Chennai (Ramachandran et al, 2002; Chhatwal et al, 2004; Kaur et al, 2008).

[D] Comparison with other Indian upper socioeconomic children

A rising trend in the prevalence of obesity in childhood and adolescence has been noted in several studies abroad (Popkin and Doak, 1998; Freedman et al,

1999; de Onis and Blossner, 2000; Chinn and Roberto, 2001). Table 4.2.36 summarizes studies reporting the prevalence of overweight and obesity in affluent children and adolescents from different parts of the country. The prevalence rates varied depending on diverse criteria used. The use of different criteria to establish the diagnosis of overweight and obesity makes it difficult to compare these studies with the present study.

Table 4.2.36: BMI (kg/m^2) of Indian boys and girls of upper socio-economic status

Place	Author	Year	Age (yr)	Sample size (n)		Criteria for measuring overweight/obesity	Overweight (%)		Obese (%)	
				Boys	Girls		Boys	Girls	Boys	Girls
Delhi	Kapil et al	2002	10-16	563	307	Overweight/obesity: age- and gender-specific BMI (IOTF)	23.1	27.7	8.3	5.5
Chennai	Subramanyam et al	2003	10-15	-	610	Overweight: BMI ≥ 85th percentile, obesity: BMI ≥ 95th percentile	-	9.7	-	6.2
Pune	Khadilkar et al	2004	10-15	1288	-	WHO BMI cut-offs Overweight: BMI = 25 – 29.9 kg/m^2, obese: BMI ≥ 30 kg/m^2	19.9	-	5.7	-
Amritsar	Sidhu et al	2005	10-15	323	317	Overweight: BMI ≥ 85th percentile, obesity: BMI ≥ 95th percentile	9.9	12.0	5.0	6.3
Delhi	Marwaha et al	2006	5-17	6197	6448	Overweight/obesity: age- and gender-specific BMI (IOTF)	16.8	19.0	5.6	5.7
Delhi	Sharma et al	2006	4-17	2497	1902	Overweight/obesity: age- and gender-specific BMI (IOTF)	23.7	20.7	7	4.7
Pune	Rao et al	2008	9-16	1146	1036	Overweight/obesity: age- and gender-specific BMI (IOTF)	24.7	21.3	-	-
Delhi	Kaur et al	2008	5-18	3298	3070	Overweight/obesity: age- and gender-specific BMI (IOTF)	14.7	16.0	6.5	7.1
Present study		2004-09	6-14	1898	1788	WHO 2007	Boys : 23.8% Girls: 13.8%			

The study by Subramanyam et al (2003) evaluating the prevalence of obesity in affluent girls aged 10-15 years in Chennai revealed the prevalence of obesity to be 6.2% in 1998 using the 95th percentile of BMI as cutoff. Similar results have been given by Sidhu et al among Amritsar children using the same criteria. In the present study, in a comparable age group (10-14 years) using the 95th percentile of BMI as cutoff, the prevalence of obesity was double (12.4%). Khadilkar et al

(2004) used the cutoff for BMI for overweight and obesity on the basis of the classification given by James et al (1988), which maynot be suitable for growing children.

Studies done in Delhi at various time points using IOTF cutoffs proposed by Cole et al (2000) also report high prevalence rates of overweight and obesity similar to those reported in the present study (Kapil et al 2002, Sharma et al 2006, Kaur et al 2008). However Marwaha et al (2006) reported lower prevalences of overweight and obesity among public school children of Delhi (5-17 years).

Inspite of variation in the criteria used to define overweight and obesity, all the studies suggest that there is a significant problem of childhood overweight and obesity in urban India.

To sum up the findings on BMI of the present study subjects:

- The median BMI of girls was higher than that of boys until age 8+ years after which BMI of both boys and girls were similar; the median BMI of boys crosses that of the girls at age 12+ years; by age 14+, median BMI of boys was 0.8 kg/m^2 higher as compared to BMI of girls.
- The peak increase in annual BMI gain was seen at 10+ years in girls and 11+ years in boys.
- BMI of both boys and girls in the present study were higher than the CDC 2000 and were way above the WHO 2007 references for all the ages.
- Using either of the references, CDC 2000 or WHO 2007, the prevalence of under-nutrition was less than 2% among boys and girls in the present study.
- WHO 2007 was realized to be a better reference in identifying over-nourished subjects compared to CDC 2000; the prevalence of over-nutrition was higher when WHO 2007 reference was used in both boys (23.8% vs. 16.2%) and girls (13.8% vs. 9.3%) compared to CDC 2000.

- High over-nutrition rates were seen in children as early as 6 years. About 22.4 % boys and 15.0% girls studying in class I (6+ years) were over-nourished using the WHO 2007 reference.
- Prevalence of over-nutrition among girls was high right from 6+ years and remained high during the pubertal age group. It decreased marginally in the post pubertal period. Among boys over-nutrition rates were high during the prepubertal years by either reference and decreased with increasing age.
- Over-nutrition rates were higher in boys (23.8%) as compared to girls (13.8%).
- The present study highlights a high prevalence of over-nutrition among children and adolescents studying in private schools in Delhi from early age. Similar trend has been reported in several other studies from within the country.

4.2.4 Circumferences

The three circumferences measured were MUAC, waist and hip circumferences. The means and standard deviations of the three circumferences of the subjects are given in Tables 4.2.37-4.2.42 and the median MUAC, waist and hip circumferences of the subjects are shown in Figures 4.2.36, 4.2.39 and 4.2.40. Details regarding percentiles are given in Annexures 8D, 8E and 8F for MUAC, waist and hip circumferences respectively.

MUAC

The mean MUAC of boys and girls in the present study ranged from 18.7±2.6 cm to 25.4 ± 3.9 cm and 19.0 ± 2.4 cm to 21.1 ± 3.1 cm respectively (Tables 4.2.37 and 4.2.38). There was a progressive increase in MUAC of boys with age, the gain being 6.9 cm between 6-14 years. In girls, MUAC increased up till 12+ years and declined thereafter. At age 6+ years, girls had a slightly higher MUAC as compared to boys, but at age 14+ years, boys had a higher MUAC, the difference being 4.3 cm.

Table 4.2.37: MUAC (cm) of boys (n=1875)			
Age (yr)	n	Mean ± SD	Δ MUAC/yr
6+	211	18.7 ± 2.6	-
7+	200	19.7 ± 2.8	1.1
8+	212	20.4 ± 3.1	0.7
9+	205	21.4 ± 3.2	0.9
10+	201	22.3 ± 3.3	0.9
11+	202	23.4 ± 3.5	1.0
12+	205	23.8 ± 4.0	0.4
13+	237	24.7 ± 3.6	0.9
14+	202	25.6 ± 3.8	0.8

Table 4.2.38: MUAC (cm) of girls (n=1766)			
Age (yr)	n	Mean ± SD	Δ MUAC/yr
6+	200	19.0 ± 2.4	-
7+	224	19.6 ± 2.6	0.6
8+	202	20.6 ± 2.8	1.0
9+	214	20.9 ± 2.7	0.2
10+	201	22.5 ± 3.3	1.6
11+	200	22.7 ± 3.1	0.3
12+	170	24.1 ± 3.2	1.4
13+	188	23.7 ± 3.3	-0.4
14+	167	21.1 ± 3.1	-2.7

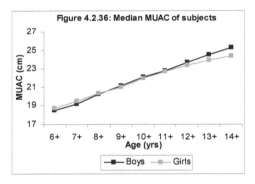

Figure 4.2.36: Median MUAC of subjects

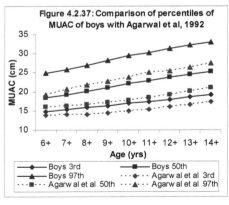

Figure 4.2.37: Comparison of percentiles of MUAC of boys with Agarwal et al, 1992

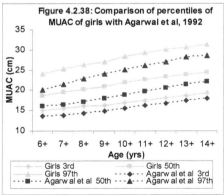

Figure 4.2.38: Comparison of percentiles of MUAC of girls with Agarwal et al, 1992

Figure 4.2.36 shows that the median MUAC of both boys and girls were comparable till the age of 11+ years, after which the median MUAC in boys continued to increase and was higher than the MUAC of girls.

The 3rd, 50th and 97th percentiles of MUAC of boys and girls of present study (Annexure 8D) were compared with those reported by Agarwal et al (1992) for 6-14 year old affluent children (Figures 4.2.37 and 4.2.38). The boys and girls in the present study had much higher MUAC than children studied 15 years ago by Agarwal et al (1992).

Waist and hip circumferences

The mean waist circumference of boys was higher while the mean hip circumference was lower than that of girls at all ages (Tables 4.2.39-4.2.42). The mean waist and hip circumferences of boys showed a spurt at 11+ years which was also the time of peak height and weight gain in boys of the present study and then remained high till 14+ years.

In girls, peak increase in annual waist and hip gain was seen at 10+ years, similar to the time of peak height and weight gain in the girls of the present study. The annual increase in waist and hip again showed a spurt again at 12+ years; thereafter it plateaued.

Figures 4.2.39 and 4.2.40 show the median waist and hip circumferences of both boys and girls. Girls had a smaller median waist and a higher hip circumference as compared to boys. At the upper end of the age range, the curves tended to plateau in girls, whereas in boys they continued to increase, and this probably reflected the different timings of the onset of puberty and gender-specific influences on waist circumference

Table 4.2.39: WC (cm) of boys (n=1863)

Age (yr)	n	Mean ± SD	Δ WC/yr
6+	209	54.4 ± 6.1	-
7+	199	57.6 ± 6.5	3.2
8+	212	59.9 ± 8.1	2.4
9+	205	61.5 ± 7.8	1.6
10+	201	64.4 ± 8.9	2.9
11+	202	68.3 ± 9.8	3.9
12+	203	69.3 ± 10.7	1.0
13+	231	71.6 ± 9.9	2.3
14+	201	73.8 ± 10.5	2.2

WC: waist circumference

Table 4.2.40: WC (cm) of girls (n=1463)

Age (yr)	n	Mean ± SD	Δ WC/yr
6+	162	52.9 ± 5.8	-
7+	189	56.3 ± 6.1	3.3
8+	179	58.0 ± 6.8	1.8
9+	190	59.2 ± 6.8	1.2
10+	148	64.5 ± 9.6	5.3
11+	190	64.6 ± 8.1	0.2
12+	137	67.2 ± 8.1	2.5
13+	130	65.3 ± 7.5	1.9
14+	138	67.9 ± 7.7	2.7

WC: waist circumference

Table 4.2.41: HC (cm) of boys (n=1863)

Age (yr)	n	Mean ± SD	Δ HC/yr
6+	209	62.4 ± 6.0	-
7+	199	66.7 ± 6.8	4.4
8+	212	69.4 ± 7.3	2.7
9+	205	71.8 ± 7.2	2.4
10+	201	75.2 ± 8.1	3.4
11+	202	79.9 ± 8.9	4.7
12+	203	82.6 ± 9.9	2.7
13+	231	86.4 ± 8.8	3.8
14+	201	89.3 ± 9.7	2.9

HC: hip circumference

Table 4.2.42: HC (cm) of girls (n=1463)

Age (yr)	n	Mean ± SD	Δ HC/yr
6+	162	63.2 ± 6.7	-
7+	189	66.8 ± 6.4	3.6
8+	179	69.8 ± 6.5	3.1
9+	190	72.1 ± 6.7	2.2
10+	148	79.1 ± 10.2	7.1
11+	190	80.8 ± 7.9	1.7
12+	137	86.1 ± 8.3	5.3
13+	130	86.7 ± 7.3	0.6
14+	138	89.8 ± 7.9	3.1

HC: hip circumference

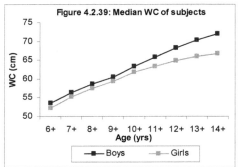

Figure 4.2.39: Median WC of subjects

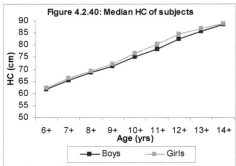

Figure 4.2.40: Median HC of subjects

During growth, body fat is laid down both subcutaneously and intra-abdominally, hence obtaining information on waist circumference may be useful in identifying overweight and obese children (Panjikkaran and Kumari 2009). The waist-to-hip ratio has been used extensively in adults. Studies published in the 1990s suggest that waist circumference may be a useful and accurate index of central fat distribution both in adults and children (Taylor et al, 1998; Goran et al, 1998). Waist circumference percentiles have been developed for children and youth in different countries like Cuba (Martinez et al, 1994), Italy (Zannolli and Morgese, 1996), Spain (Moreno et al, 1999), United Kingdom (McCarthy et al, 2001) and Canada (Katzmarzyk, 2004) and different cutoffs for example 90th, 75th, 97th percentiles have been used. However, there has been no consensus on the globally applicable standards for use in identifying children and adolescents with abdominal obesity.

Waist circumference percentiles of boys and girls from the present study were compared with corresponding waist percentiles given by McCarthy et al (2001) for 5-16.9 years old UK children. In both the studies, waist circumference percentiles were constructed and smoothened using the LMS method and the site of the waist measurement was defined identically i.e. the lowest circumference between the costal margin and iliac crest (natural waist). Studies by Clasey et al (1999) and Lean et al (1995) found that waist circumference measured at the narrowest point of the torso is a strong predictor of total adipose tissue and visceral adipose tissue measured with computed tomography.

Figures 4.2.41 and 4.2.42 show that there was an increase in the waist circumference of boys up till 14+ years of age. The 50th and 95th percentiles of boys in the present study were higher than respective UK percentiles for all ages while the 5th percentile was close to the UK 5th percentile. In girls, the 5th percentile of girls coincided, 50th percentile was slightly above and 95th percentile was way above that of UK percentiles. Percentile distribution of waist circumference for the present study subjects is given in Annexure 8E.

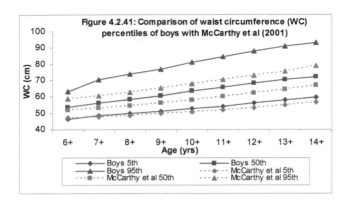

Figure 4.2.41: Comparison of waist circumference (WC) percentiles of boys with McCarthy et al (2001)

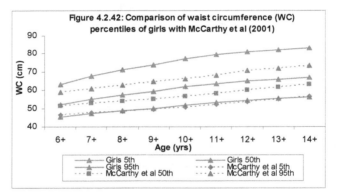

Figure 4.2.42: Comparison of waist circumference (WC) percentiles of girls with McCarthy et al (2001)

To sum up the findings on circumferences of subjects in the present study:

- The median MUAC of both boys and girls were comparable till the age of 11+ years, after which the median MUAC in boys continued to increase and was higher than the MUAC of girls.
- In girls, MUAC increased up till 12+ years and declined thereafter.
- The 3rd, 50th and 97th percentiles of MUAC of boys and girls of present study were higher than the 3rd, 50th and 97th percentiles reported by Agarwal et al (1992) for 6-14 year old affluent children.

- Girls had a smaller median waist and a higher hip circumference as compared to boys.
- The mean waist and hip circumferences of boys showed a spurt at around 11+ years in boys and then remained high till 14+ years. In girls, peak increase in annual waist and hip gain was seen at 10+ years and again at 12+ years; thereafter it plateaued.
- Waist circumference percentiles of both boys and girls in the present study were higher than the waist percentile charts given by McCarthy et al (2001) for UK children for all the ages.

4.2.5 Fatfolds

The four fatfolds measured were triceps, biceps, subscapular and suprailiac. Details regarding percentiles of each are given in Appendices 8G-8J.

Triceps and biceps fatfolds

Tables 4.2.43-4.2.46 indicates that right from the age of 6+ years, girls had higher mean triceps and biceps as compared to boys. In boys, velocities for triceps and biceps fatfold thickness was positive in the earlier years, with a peak at about 10-11 years; then velocity declined and actually became negative. This is because of the enlargement of the underlying muscular tissue (Parthmanthan and Prakash, 1994). The total gain in triceps and biceps thicknesses during the age period 6-14 years was lower in boys (4.3 mm and 1.3 mm) as compared to girls (5.3 mm and 1.6 mm). At the age of 14+ years the differences between the mean triceps and biceps of girls and boys was 3.2 mm and 1.1 mm respectively (Tables 4.2.43 and 4.2.44).

The median triceps and biceps fatfolds in boys and girls are given in Figures 4.2.43 and 4.2.44. There was a progressive increase in both triceps and biceps with increasing age in girls. Among boys both the fatfolds increased steadily till the age group of 11+ years and thereafter gradually decreased. Both triceps and biceps were higher in girls as compared to boys. This difference widened after 10+ years because around puberty girls accumulate fat.

Table 4.2.43: Triceps (mm) of boys (n=1856)

Age (yr)	n	Mean ± SD	Δ triceps/yr
6+	209	9.9 ± 4.3	-
7+	198	11.1 ± 4.9	1.1
8+	212	12.3 ± 6.2	1.2
9+	205	12.5 ± 5.3	0.2
10+	200	13.6 ± 6.2	1.1
11+	201	15.3 ± 6.4	1.7
12+	202	14.9 ± 5.6	-0.3
13+	230	14.8 ± 6.9	-0.2
14+	199	14.2 ± 6.5	-0.6

Table 4.2.44: Triceps (mm) of girls (n=1758)

Age (yr)	n	Mean ± SD	Δ triceps/yr
6+	200	12.1 ± 4.5	-
7+	224	11.9 ± 4.3	-0.3
8+	202	13.5 ± 5.0	1.6
9+	213	13.8 ± 4.9	0.4
10+	197	15.4 ± 5.9	1.5
11+	199	15.3 ± 5.6	-0.1
12+	170	16.8 ± 5.9	1.5
13+	188	16.3 ± 6.4	-0.5
14+	165	17.4 ± 6.2	1.1

Table 4.2.45: Biceps (mm) of boys (n=1856)

Age (yr)	n	Mean ± SD	Δ biceps/yr
6+	209	7.2 ± 3.6	-
7+	198	7.4 ± 3.9	0.2
8+	212	7.9 ± 4.3	0.5
9+	205	7.9 ± 3.8	0.0
10+	200	9.2 ± 5.1	1.3
11+	201	10.3 ± 5.2	1.1
12+	202	9.2 ± 4.4	-1.1
13+	230	9.2 ± 4.9	-0.1
14+	199	8.5 ± 4.7	-0.7

Table 4.2.46: Biceps (mm) of girls (n=1758)

Age (yr)	n	Mean ± SD	Δ biceps/yr
6+	200	8.0 ± 3.1	-
7+	224	7.3 ± 2.7	-0.7
8+	202	7.7 ± 3.3	0.5
9+	213	8.7 ± 3.5	1.0
10+	197	9.9 ± 4.4	1.2
11+	199	9.6 ± 4.1	-0.3
12+	170	10.4 ± 4.6	0.8
13+	188	9.7 ± 4.4	-0.6
14+	165	9.6 ± 4.3	-0.1

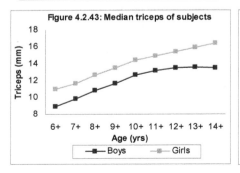

Figure 4.2.43: Median triceps of subjects

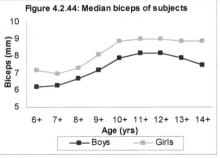

Figure 4.2.44: Median biceps of subjects

Subscapular and suprailiac fatfolds

Mean subscapular and suprailiac fatfold thickness of girls was higher than that of boys for all ages (Tables 4.2.47 - 4.2.50). The mean subscapular thickness of boys increased till the age of 11+ years; after which the values declined. This is due to the fact that around puberty boys become muscular. The total gain in subscapular and suprailiac thickness was 5.8 mm and 7.3 mm in boys during the age period 6-14 years. Girls showed a higher gain, the increase being 6.2 mm and 6.7 mm, respectively. At the age of 14 years the differences between mean subscapular and suprailiac of boys and girls was 2.1 mm and 1.5 mm respectively.

Table 4.2.47: Subscapular (SS; mm) of boys (n=1856)

Age (yr)	n	Mean ± SD	Δ SS/yr
6+	209	7.8 ± 4.51	-
7+	198	8.4 ± 4.8	0.6
8+	212	9.9 ± 7.5	1.5
9+	205	11.0 ± 6.5	1.1
10+	200	12.4 ± 7.8	1.4
11+	201	14.9 ± 9.0	2.5
12+	202	14.8 ± 9.4	-0.1
13+	230	13.9 ± 7.6	-0.9
14+	199	13.6 ± 7.5	-0.3

Table 4.2.48: Subscapular (SS; mm) of girls (n=1453)

Age (yr)	n	Mean ± SD	Δ SS/yr
6+	162	9.4 ± 5.0	-
7+	189	10.1 ± 5.1	0.7
8+	179	11.1 ± 5.9	1.0
9+	190	12.7 ± 6.5	1.6
10+	143	14.7 ± 7.4	2.0
11+	188	15.0 ± 7.3	0.3
12+	137	17.2 ± 7.4	2.2
13+	129	14.5 ± 6.3	-2.7
14+	136	15.7 ± 6.2	1.2

Table 4.2.49: Suprailiac (SI; mm) of boys

Age (yr)	n	Mean ± SD	Δ SI/yr
6+	209	8.2 ± 5.7	-
7+	198	8.9 ± 6.1	0.6
8+	211	10.3 ± 8.5	1.4
9+	205	10.7 ± 6.8	0.4
10+	200	13.2 ± 8.5	2.5
11+	200	14.6 ± 8.8	1.4
12+	201	14.1 ± 8.7	-0.5
13+	230	15.7 ± 8.7	1.6
14+	197	15.6 ± 8.6	-0.1

Table 4.2.50: Suprailiac (SI; mm) of girls

Age (yr)	n	Mean ± SD	Δ SI/yr
6+	162	10.4 ± 5.6	-
7+	189	9.3 ± 4.8	-1.0
8+	179	11.2 ± 7.8	1.8
9+	190	12.3 ± 6.7	1.1
10+	142	14.6 ± 7.9	2.4
11+	188	14.9 ± 7.0	0.3
12+	137	16.6 ± 7.4	1.8
13+	130	14.8 ± 6.3	-1.8
14+	136	17.1 ± 6.6	2.3

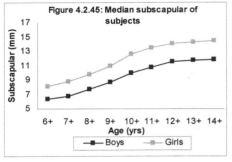
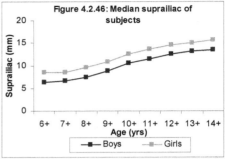

The median subscapular and suprailiac fatfolds in boys and girls shows that both subscapular and suprailiac fatfolds were higher in girls as compared to boys (Figures 4.2.45 and 4.2.46).

The observation that girls had higher fatfolds than boys beyond 11 yrs of age is in confirmation with other reported studies from India (Agarwal et al, 1992; Vijayraghavan et al, 1974; Kapoor et al, 1991; Rao et al, 2008) as well as from other populations (Must A, 1991). Inspite of somewhat higher MUAC in the age group 12+ years and beyond (Figure 4.2.35) boys had lower fat fold thickness as compared to girls beyond 12+ years. These results are consistent with greater gains in muscle and bone experienced by boys and greater gains in total body fat experienced by girls during adolescence (Sardinha et al, 1999).

[A] Comparison with international standards

Triceps and subscapular fatfolds

A comparison of the 5th, 50th and 95th percentiles of triceps and subscapular fatfold thickness of present study boys and girls with corresponding centiles reported from NHANES I (1971-74; 9-14 years) showed that boys and girls in the present study had substantially higher values especially for subscapular fatfolds, as compared to NHANES I for all the percentiles (5th, 50th and 95th) (Figures 4.2.47-4.2.50).

These data suggest that public school children in Delhi have higher fatfolds especially truncal fatfolds as compared to US children in NHANES I. Percentile distribution of triceps and subscapular fatfolds for the present study are given in Annexures 8G and 8I.

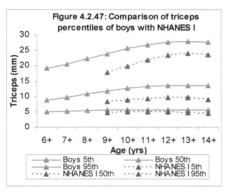

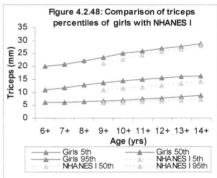

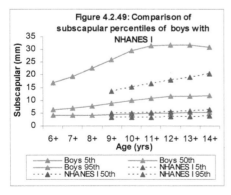

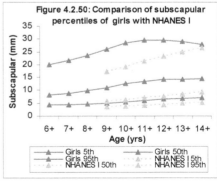

[B] Prevalence of obesity using triceps fatfolds

Prevalence of obesity using triceps fatfold thickness was estimated using cutoffs proposed by Lohman and Going (2006) where boys with an estimated triceps fatfold thickness of 22 mm and girls with an estimated thickness of 27 mm were considered obese. Figure 4.2.51 depicts the prevalence of obesity in boys and girls. Prevalence of obesity was 3.4% in girls while it was marginally high in boys (11.2%).

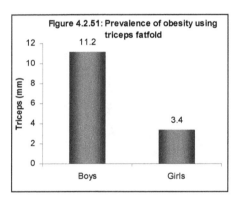

To sum up the findings on fatfolds of subjects in the present study:

- All the four fatfolds were higher in case of girls as compared to boys right from the age of 6+ years.
- Among boys fatfolds increased steadily till the age of 11+ years and plateaued thereafter while in girls, fatfolds continued to increase with increase in age.
- Obesity rates based on triceps cutoffs were 11.2% in boys and 3.4% in girls.
- Comparison of the 5th, median and 95th percentiles of triceps and subscapular fatfolds of boys and girls with corresponding percentile values from NHANES I showed that boys and girls both had higher values as compared to NHANES I for all the percentiles.

4.3 BODY FAT ESTIMATION

Of the total 3686 subjects enrolled for the study, estimation of body fat was done in a selected sub sample (n=1220) of 667 boys and 553 girls. The amount of body fat was assessed using two techniques: anthropometry (using multiple fatfolds) and BIA.

BIA was done at two schools which had the essential infrastructure i.e. an enclosed room with a wooden bed in which the child could lie down and rest for 10 minutes, after which the device was switched on and the impedance value calculated by the manufacturer's software was recorded. Table 4.3.1 gives the age and sex wise distribution of subjects for BIA. The four fatfold thicknesses (triceps, biceps, subscapular and suprailiac) of these subjects were measured as a part of the anthropometric assessment.

Table 4.3.1: Age and sex wise distribution of subjects for BIA			
Age (yrs)	Boys	Girls	Total
6+	51	47	98
7+	64	74	138
8+	67	62	129
9+	108	95	203
10+	63	53	116
11+	85	65	150
12+	61	46	107
13+	107	52	159
14+	61	59	120
Total	**667**	**553**	**1220**

There was no significant difference in the anthropometric characteristics of the total sample (n=3686) and the sub sample (n=1220) on whom body fat was estimated (Table not shown).

4.3.1 Techniques for body fat estimation

There are several methods available for measurement of body fat, ranging from those that actually measure body components to those that predict them. The former are costly and can only be used in well-equipped laboratories, usually on small number of subjects. Therefore FM is usually measured by more simple predictive measures such as anthropometry using fatfolds and bioimpedance (BIA) which offer a two compartment measure of FM and FFM.

In the present study also, body fat was determined using fatfolds and BIA, which indirectly measure body density and body water respectively. Both anthropometry and BIA are indirect, simple methods to assess body fat; however it is not clear whether the results of these techniques are comparable. In the present study, fat mass of 1220 subjects was estimated by the two techniques and the results were compared.

Many race, age and sex specific equations exist for the estimation of body fat from fatfolds as well as from BIA in children. Inspite of the fact that there are good reasons to believe that the body fat and its distribution in Indian children may differ from the Caucasians, so far no equation for deriving FM from anthropometric indices or BIA have been developed in India and validated against gold standards such as DEXA. Because of this, FM was computed from BIA and anthropometry (fatfolds) using various equations developed for Caucasian children.

Since age or maturational state has been identified as an important predictive variable of body composition (Slaughter et al, 1988; Reilly et al, 1995), equations specific to the age range covered in the present study were selected. Table 4.3.2 summarizes the prediction equations selected based on BIA and anthropometry (fatfolds). All these equations were applied to the subjects and FM was derived.

Table 4.3.2: Prediction equations for FM estimation	
Technique	Equation
Fat fold thickness	Slaughter et al, 1988
	Johnston et al, 1988
BIA	Houtkooper et al, 1992
	Deurenberg et al, 1991
	Schaefer et al, 1994
	Kushner et al, 1992

Comparison of the mean FM values computed from the two fatfold based equations on the same children is given in Table 4.3.3. The computed FM values were significantly different (p<0.05) using the two equations. Similarly, mean FM values computed using the four BIA based equations also gave significantly different estimates of FM and the data is shown in Table 4.3.4.

Table 4.3.3: Mean fat mass (kg) using different fatfold equations (8-14 yrs)			
Group	Johnston et al, 1988	Slaughter et al, 1988	p-Value
Boys (n=552)	6.50 ± 5.3	12.01 ± 8.0	0.001
Girls (n=432)	8.28 ± 4.5	12.44 ± 6.5	0.001

Reported values are means ± SD; p<0.05 is statistically significant; Paired t-test

Table 4.3.4: Mean fat mass (kg) using different BIA equations (6-14 yrs)				
Group	Houtkooper et al, 1992	Deurenberg et al, 1991	Schaefer et al, 1994	Kushner et al, 1992
Boys (n=667)	9.8 ± 6.1	11.0 ± 5.4	12.6 ± 8.3	13.1 ± 7.2
Girls (n=553)	10.2 ± 5.7	11.7 ± 5.0	13.0 ± 7.4	12.1 ± 6.6

Reported values are means ± SD; p<0.05 is statistically significant; One way ANOVA followed by paired t-test (critical difference)

The mean FM from all the six equations on all 1220 subjects (6-14 years) has been compared in Figure 4.3.1.

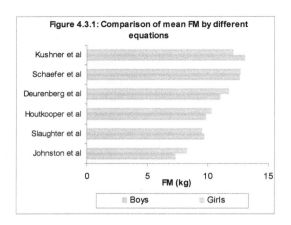

Figure 4.3.1: Comparison of mean FM by different equations

Comparison of the FM values computed from BIA based equations with those derived from anthropometry (fatfolds) was difficult as there were substantial differences in body FM computed using different formulae (Figure 4.3.1), with Kushner's and Schaefer's equation (both based on BIA) giving the highest FM in boys and girls respectively and Johnston's equation (based on fatfolds) giving the lowest mean FM. The variations in FM computed by various methods are to be expected because of methodological differences. The most obvious difference between the samples recruited in these studies was age; equation of Kushner et al (1992) was based on a broad age range (0.02 months to 67 years) and so the difference in FM was not surprising. Body density was predicted from four fatfolds (triceps, biceps, subscapular and suprailiac) in the equation by Johnston et al while body fat percent was predicted using two fatfolds in Slaughter et al (1988) study. However, Deurenberg et al (1990) has reported that the prediction error in deriving percent body fat from four fatfolds is only slightly lower than that from only two fatfolds. This observation has also been reported by other workers in adults (Durnin and Womersley, 1974) and in elderly (Deurenberg et al, 1989). Equations by Houtkooper et al (1992) and Kushner et al (1992) used the resistance index (Ht^2/R) along with weight as predicting variable while Deurenberg et al (1991) included height and sex also; Schaefer et al (1994) equation has Ht^2/R and age as the prediction variables. The different approaches may have introduced the differences in FM. Of all the equations, mean FM values derived using Houtkooper et al (1992; based on BIA) and Slaughter et al (1988; based on fatfold anthropometry) were closest.

Thus, the prediction equation chosen can have a profound effect on the estimate obtained, and hence care is required in deciding which equation to use. In view of the well-documented differences in body composition (fat and muscle mass) between Indians and Caucasians, it may not be appropriate to use any of these equations to compute FM and FFM in Indians. Since there is no Indian equation available based on either of the techniques, the investigator had no choice but to derive body fat using these Caucasian equations.

[A] Selection of equations

In order to select one equation from each of the two field methods, all the equations selected based on the two techniques were applied to the 17 children on whom validation using D_2O was done (given in section 3.6). The mean FM and %BF are given in Table 4.3.5. Details of the data are given in Annexure 9.

Table 4.3.5: Mean FM and %BF derived from D_2O and different equations based on BIA and fatfolds		
Technique used	FM (kg) (n=17)	% BF (n=17)
D_2O (Criterion method)	4.7 ± 1.8	18.6 ± 5.1
Houtkooper et al, 1992	4.4 ± 1.9	17.1 ± 4.3
Deurenberg et al, 1991	6.2 ± 1.8	25.2 ± 4.2
Schaefer et al, 1994	4.2 ± 2.7	15.7 ± 6.7
Kushner et al, 1992	6.0 ± 2.0	24.3 ± 5.6
Johnston et al, 1988	1.5 ± 1.2	5.5 ± 4.4
Slaughter et al, 1988	2.8 ± 1.3	10.9 ± 3.0
Reported values are means ± SD		

Bland and Altman analysis was also done for FM (kg) from each of the equations against D_2O as the criterion method (Figure 4.3.2 and 4.3.3). The results are also shown in Table 4.3.6.

Table 4.3.6: Results of the Bland and Altman analysis for FM (kg) using D_2O as the criteria

Technique	Bias (kg)	r	p-Value	ICC á	Limits of agreement
D_2O vs. Houtkooper et al, 1992	0.27	+0.91	0.001	0.95	(-1.4, +1.9)
D_2O vs. Deurenberg et al, 1991	-1.53	+0.91	0.001	0.95	(-3.0, +0.03)
D_2O vs. Schaefer et al, 1994	0.64	+0.84	0.001	0.87	(-2.6, +3.6)
D_2O vs. Kushner et al, 1992	-1.33	+0.92	0.001	0.95	(-2.9, +0.3)
D_2O vs. Johnston et al, 1988	3.2	+0.87	0.001	0.90	(+1.3, +5.1)
D_2O vs. Slaughter et al, 1988	1.9	+0.92	0.001	0.93	(+0.3, +3.5)

ICC: Inter class correlation

Body fatness was overestimated by the equations of Deurenberg et al and Kushner et al (Table 4.3.5). The equation of Houtkooper et al had the smallest bias and narrowest limits of agreements relative to D_2O (Table 4.3.6). The equations of Slaughter et al and Johnston et al underestimated fatness relative to D_2O, and the latter equation predicted a number of very low fatness estimates (some negative estimates). As an example of the range of estimates which were obtained from the five prediction equations in the same child, in a typical boy predicted fatness ranged from 1.1% (Johnston et al equation) to 24.0% (Deurenberg et al equation) with fatness from D_2O of 14.0%.

Houtkooper et al (1992) equation gave the smallest bias and reasonable limits of agreement as compared to the other BIA based equations. Among the two fatfold based equations, the equation given by Slaughter et al (1988) gave a lower bias (Table 4.3.6).

Thus for the present study, among the fatfold based equations, the equation devised by Slaughter et al (1988) based on triceps and subscapular fatfold thicknesses was selected as it covered the entire 6-14 year age range. The cross validity of the Slaughter et al equation has been reported to be high (Janz et al 1993) and these are effectively the 'standard' equations used in America (Reilly et al, 1995). For the assessment of body fat using BIA, the equation fed in the equipment software given by Houtkooper et al (1992) for Caucasians, was selected. Also, correlation between FM computed from equation by Houtkooper

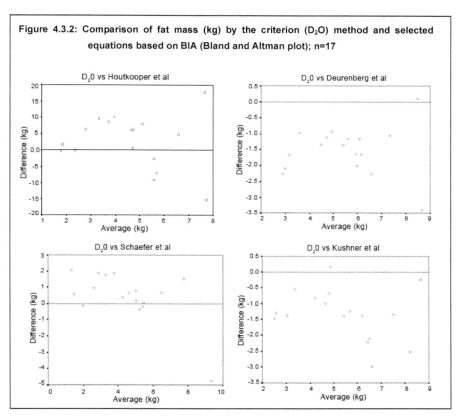

Figure 4.3.2: Comparison of fat mass (kg) by the criterion (D_2O) method and selected equations based on BIA (Bland and Altman plot); n=17

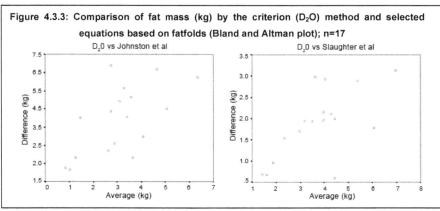

Figure 4.3.3: Comparison of fat mass (kg) by the criterion (D_2O) method and selected equations based on fatfolds (Bland and Altman plot); n=17

et al (1992) (as given in the manufacturer's software) and the new predictive equation derived as a part of validation of BIA using D_2O was +0.99 (refer section 3.6). Also for Slaughter et al (1988) and Houtkooper et al (1992) equations, the criterion method was same, a multicomponent model using body density and body water.

Both the equations were applied on the subjects and FM and %BF derived using the two techniques were compared.

[B] Comparison of techniques: fatfolds vs BIA

The estimation of FM using fatfolds and BIA was done on 1220 subjects (667 boys and 553 girls). The body composition characteristics for these 1220 subjects, grouped by age and sex, are reported in Table 4.3.7.

Table 4.3.5 shows that all the descriptive variables increased with age ($p<0.05$); with the exception of impedance which decreased with increase in age in both boys and girls ($r= -0.55$, $p<0.05$). Whole body impedance ranged from 411 to 1033 Ω with girls having higher impedance and hence higher FM as compared to boys at all age points. Girls also had significantly higher fatfolds. These differences are consistent with the greater gains in total body fat and subcutaneous adipose tissue experienced by girls during adolescence. The mean weight and height of boys was significantly higher for boys, mean BMI was not significantly different for boys and girls. Boys had a higher MUAC and waist circumference but the hip circumference did not differ significantly among the two sexes.

Comparison of mean FM computed from fatfolds (Slaughter's equation, 1988) against that computed using BIA (manufacturer's equation, Houtkooper et al, 1992) is also shown in Table 4.3.8.

Table 4.3.7: Body composition characteristics of subjects (n=1220)

Ages (yr)	n	Weight (kg)	Height (cm)	BMI (kg/m^2)	MUAC (cm)	Impedance (Ω)	Triceps (mm)	Biceps (mm)	SS (mm)	SI (mm)	WC (cm)	HC (cm)	FM (BIA)	FM (FFT)
BOYS	667	40.6±14.6	144.1±15.8	18.9±3.8	22.5±3.9	686.6±87.8	13.1±6.2	8.5±4.7	11.9±7.5	12.4±8.2	64.9±10.6	76.6±11.3	9.9±6.1	9.7±7.6
6+	51	24.7±4.9	120.4±4.9	16.9±2.6	19.2±2.5	751.3±69.6	10.0±4.4	8.1±4.5	8.5±5.2	8.2±5.3	56.2±6.6	64.0±5.8	5.3±2.8	4.6±3.1
7+	64	26.6±6.1	125.7±6.7	16.7±2.6	19.5±2.8	730.7±72.1	9.4±3.9	6.0±2.5	7.6±3.8	7.0±3.9	57.0±6.6	66.4±8.1	5.2±3.0	4.5±3.0
8+	67	29.8±6.4	131.6±6.4	17.0±2.5	20.3±2.9	731.4±72.9	10.3±4.4	6.2±2.9	8.0±4.4	8.1±5.2	59.4±6.8	68.8±6.9	6.4±3.0	5.5±3.4
9+	108	32.8±7.0	136.5±6.2	17.5±2.8	21.4±3.4	724.5±65.8	11.7±4.8	7.2±2.9	9.9±5.0	9.9±6.0	60.9±7.8	71.2±7.3	7.4±3.5	7.0±4.1
10+	63	39.9±9.4	143.2±6.5	19.3±3.5	23.0±3.3	700.8±83.6	15.2±5.7	10.6±5.5	13.9±8.0	14.7±8.5	66.4±9.5	76.9±8.1	10.5±5.5	10.9±6.9
11+	85	42.8±9.8	147.9±6.6	19.4±3.6	23.2±3.6	694.0±67.0	14.9±5.8	10.6±5.7	13.9±7.7	14.3±8.8	67.6±9.7	79.2±8.5	11.3±5.5	11.2±6.6
12+	61	52.0±13.4	155.6±9.3	21.3±4.0	25.0±4.0	645.3±82.8	15.7±6.8	9.9±4.8	16.3±10.0	15.8±8.6	72.1±10.7	85.2±10.1	14.1±7.1	14.9±9.8
13+	107	55.0±11.5	160.9±9.0	21.2±3.6	25.1±3.6	612.0±76.2	15.2±7.0	9.6±5.1	14.7±8.0	16.1±8.6	71.7±8.9	86.8±7.7	13.5±6.6	14.3±8.5
14+	61	55.2±11.9	164.6±8.4	20.3±3.7	24.6±3.7	615.2±71.0	14.4±7.6	8.2±5.0	12.8±7.6	15.3±9.1	69.2±12.4	85.3±9.6	12.4±7.3	12.4±8.9
GIRLS	553	37.6±12.7	139.9±13.8	18.7±3.6	21.7±3.3	741.0±90.4	14.3±5.7	8.6±4.0	13.1±6.9	13.1±7.6	61.1±8.3	76.3±11.1	10.3±5.9	9.9±6.2
6+	47	24.9±5.7	120.3±6.2	17.1±2.6	19.4±2.4	795.5±88.0	12.1±4.0	7.4±2.4	9.7±5.1	10.0±5.4	54.9±6.4	65.2±6.8	6.2±2.5	5.2±2.7
7+	74	26.0±5.4	124.7±6.2	16.6±2.6	19.7±2.5	777.2±85.9	10.9±3.9	6.6±2.4	9.8±5.2	8.8±4.2	55.8±6.0	66.5±6.2	5.8±2.7	5.1±2.8
8+	62	29.4±6.3	130.7±6.4	17.1±2.8	20.4±2.9	776.6±65.3	12.1±4.6	6.6±2.8	9.6±5.4	10.3±10.0	58.3±6.9	70.0±6.6	7.1±3.5	6.0±3.1
9+	95	32.2±7.0	135.0±6.4	17.5±3.0	20.8±2.8	776.7±83.2	13.7±5.4	8.6±3.7	12.9±7.3	11.9±7.0	58.5±7.1	71.8±6.8	8.3±3.7	7.8±4.3
10+	53	36.9±7.8	142.4±6.0	18.1±3.0	21.4±2.7	748.8±88.1	14.0±5.3	8.7±3.4	13.4±6.2	12.9±6.9	61.4±6.8	75.8±7.6	10.6±6.7	9.1±4.5
11+	65	43.0±9.4	147.1±7.3	19.7±3.3	22.4±2.9	707.2±75.8	15.8±5.5	10.1±4.5	15.1±6.5	15.3±7.0	64.5±7.5	81.2±7.4	12.0±4.9	11.6±5.4
12+	46	50.4±9.3	152.8±5.8	21.6±3.8	24.1±3.1	666.9±55.3	17.0±6.1	10.4±5.5	17.4±7.8	17.8±7.1	67.0±7.4	86.2±8.3	15.0±5.6	14.6±6.8
13+	52	49.8±9.3	155.8±5.4	20.5±5.4	23.6±2.9	679.8±83.9	16.2±6.1	9.5±4.1	14.6±6.7	16.0±7.5	65.1±7.9	85.9±7.1	13.9±5.4	13.3±6.1
14+	59	53.2±9.8	157.1±5.0	21.6±3.9	24.7±3.4	690.8±69.9	18.1±7.3	10.1±4.9	16.6±6.5	17.2±6.7	67.9±7.6	89.7±9.0	16.5±6.4	15.5±7.3
p-value		0.001	0.001	0.071	0.001	0.001	0.001	0.001	0.001	0.001	0.001	0.52	0.001	0.50

Reported values are expressed as mean ± SD. $p<0.05$ is statistically significant. Student's t-test

131

Table 4.3.8: Comparison of FM (kg) using fatfolds and BIA		
FM (kg)	Boys (n=667)	Girls (n=553)
Fatfolds	9.7 ± 7.6	9.9 ± 6.2
BIA	9.9 ± 6.1	10.3 ± 5.9
Reported values are expressed as mean ± SD, p= NS; Paired t-test		

The values of FM computed from fatfolds were lower as compared to FM computed from BIA in both boys and girls. This is because fatfold thickness measurements provide information only on subcutaneous FM while BIA provides information on FM including visceral FM. Therefore, it is logical that BIA derived FM values should be higher than FM values by fatfold thicknesses. In this study, values of FM computed from the two techniques were not significantly different in both boys and girls. Girls had a higher FM than boys using either of the two techniques.

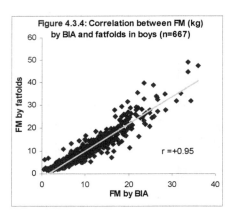
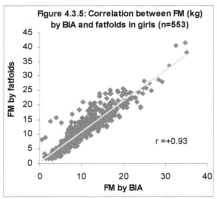

There was a strong correlation between FM measured by the two field techniques, fatfolds and BIA in both boys (r=+0.95; 95% CI=0.94-0.96) and girls (r=+0.93, 95% CI= 0.93-0.94) (Figures 4.3.4 and 4.3.5).

The methods that yield estimates with high correlation coefficient may not necessarily show a degree of agreement (Bland and Altman, 1986). Therefore the difference in estimates of FM (kg) obtained via BIA and fatfolds was plotted against the average FM (kg) of the two techniques, together for boys and girls. Figure 4.3.6 provides the corresponding Bland and Altman plot.

Figure 4.3.6: Comparison of fat mass by BIA and fatfolds (Bland and Altman plot); n=1220

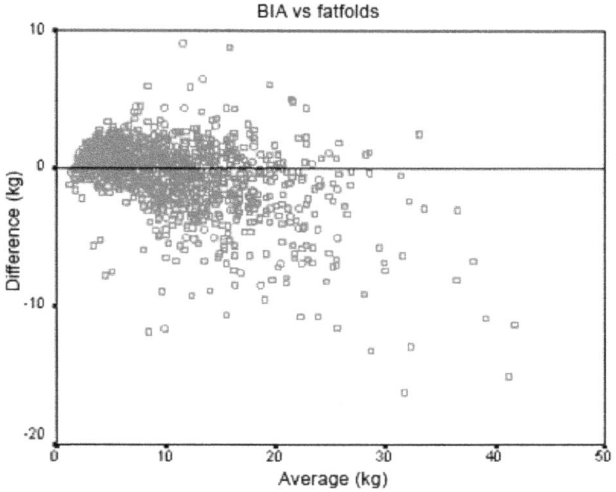

The results of the statistical analysis (Bland and Altman, 1986) are shown in Table 4.3.9. The mean bias predicted was low (-0.4%) and the 1.96 SD ranged from (-5.6) to (+4.8) supporting the overall equivalence of the two techniques.

Table 4.3.9: Results of the Bland and Altman analysis (n=1220)						
BIA (Mean±SD)	Fatfolds (Mean±SD)	Bias (kg)	r	p-Value	ICC á	Limits of agreement
10.0±5.9	10.4±7.1	-0.4	+0.94	0.001	0.96	(-5.6, +4.8)
ICC: Inter class correlation						

Both fatfold anthropometry and BIA are indirect methods of assessing body composition. All indirect methods result in errors of prediction. Anthropometry can give an error of 3.0% to 9.0% (Vansant et al, 1994), although Lukaski et al (1986) reported an error of about 2.7% with BIA.

Fatfolds are the most widely used technique to measure body fat in epidemiologic studies. Various sites of measurement have been suggested, and probably the best established and frequently reported are biceps, triceps subscapular and suprailiac. These fatfold measurements when applied to race, age and sex specific prediction equations give information on the amount of fat in the body. In addition to total fat, it is also possible to assess the distribution of fat especially if circumferential measurements (MUAC, waist and hip circumference) are also measured. This method, however, has two limitations. Accurate fatfold measurements require trained skilled nutritionists/ anthropologists; not all those who get trained develop the needed accuracy. In thin and obese individuals measurements of skin fold thickness is often difficult; even in the hands of skilled nutritionists the measurements may not be very accurate. However, this might not be feasible in large-scale surveys. Variation in the compressibility and the fat content of subcutaneous tissues as well as the thickness of the skin are additional sources of error.

BIA gives an accurate estimate of FM and is a simpler, quicker procedure, which does not require highly skilled investigators; in addition, BIA involves less interobserver variation than do fatfold measurements (Horlick et al, 2002). It is a useful technique for body composition analysis in healthy individuals and in those with a number of chronic conditions such as obesity, diabetes mellitus and other medical conditions in which major disturbances of water distribution are not present. BIA may be a useful and alternative method for detecting body composition in children and for measuring the amount of fat in pediatric populations. However, BIA doesnot give any information regarding the distribution of fat. Earlier studies have reported both under and overestimation of body fat by impedance measurements as compared to DEXA (Sung et al, 2001; Vasudev et al, 2004). These differences might relate to the different impedance devices used and the in-built unknown prediction equations which could also result in measurement differences between different machines. Prediction equations for body composition tend to be population-specific due to differences in predictors among population groups.

In conclusion there was a good agreement between the two techniques for measurement of body fat, fatfolds and BIA, although each has its own advantages and disadvantages. Accurate measurement of fat fold thickness can be done only by highly skilled trained persons. BIA does not require such highly skilled persons. Both techniques have potential for widespread use because of their simplicity and low cost. In view of the importance of body fat as a determinant of risk of diabetes and cardiovascular disease in adult life, it is essential that assessment of body fat and its distribution is taken up as a component of nutrition assessment in children especially from affluent urban segments of population in India. If the examination or the survey is being done by trained nutritionists/anthropologists, then circumferential and fatfold thickness measurements can be used for assessment of FM. If however, the surveys are being done by those who are not skilled in fatfold measurements, bioelectrical impedance analysis may be the preferred method for FM assessment.

To sum up the findings on techniques of body fat estimation:

- Based on the D_2O validation data, among the fatfold based equations, the equation devised by Slaughter et al (1988) based on triceps and subscapular fatfold thicknesses was selected and for the assessment of body fat using BIA, the equation fed in the equipment software given by Houtkooper et al (1992) for Caucasians, was selected.

- Mean fat mass estimated was not significantly different using the two techniques, fatfolds and BIA in boys (9.7 ± 7.6 vs. 9.9 ± 6.1; p=NS). The mean fat mass in girls was 9.9 ± 6.2 using fatfolds and 10.3 ± 5.9 using BIA and the difference was not statistically significant.

- There was a strong correlation between fat mass measured by anthropometry (using fatfolds) and BIA, in both boys (r=+0.95; 95% CI=0.94-0.96) and girls (r=+0.93; 95% CI=0.93-0.94). The Bland and Altman analysis also showed that there was good agreement between the two techniques, fatfolds and BIA.

- BIA gives an accurate estimate of fat mass and is a simpler, quicker procedure, which does not require highly skilled investigators and involves less inter-observer variation than do fatfold measurements. Hence, BIA may be a useful and alternative method for measuring the amount of fat in pediatric populations. However, BIA doesnot give any information regarding the distribution of fat.

- Both techniques have potential for widespread use because of their simplicity and low cost, although each has its own advantages and disadvantages. If the examination or the survey is being done by trained nutritionists/anthropologists, then circumferential and fatfold thickness measurements can be used for assessment of fat mass. If however, the surveys are being done by those who are not skilled in fatfold measurements, BIA may be the preferred method for fat mass assessment.

4.3.2 Fat mass index

The use of fat mass index (FMI) (FM/ht^2) has been proposed as an alternative to BMI when estimates of FM are available. This is because one of the major determinants of weight and FM is height of the individuals. In order to eliminate / reduce variations due to height, body mass index (BMI) (wt / ht^2) has been used. A similar index, FM index (FMI) (FM/ht^2) is now being suggested to assess adiposity after minimizing the effect of height on FM (Lohman and Going, 2006).

Table 4.3.10: Fat mass index (kg/m^2) of subjects

Ages (yr)	n	Boys Mean ± SD	n	Girls Mean ± SD	p-Value
6+	51	3.6 ± 1.8	47	4.2 ± 1.45	0.09
7+	64	3.3 ± 1.7	74	3.7 ± 1.58	0.12
8+	67	3.6 ± 1.5	62	4.1 ± 1.86	0.09
9+	108	3.9 ± 1.7	95	4.5 ± 1.87	0.02
10+	63	4.9 ± 2.3	53	4.7 ± 1.71	0.43
11+	85	5.1 ± 2.3	65	5.5 ± 2.10	0.24
12+	61	5.8 ± 2.9	46	6.4 ± 2.44	0.45
13+	107	5.3 ± 2.6	52	6.0 ± 2.15	0.01
14+	61	4.7 ± 2.6	59	6.7 ± 2.60	0.02

p<0.05 is statistically significant; Student's t-test

Thus, FMI has been calculated; age wise means and standard deviations are shown in Table 4.3c.1. For a given age, girls had a higher FM and therefore a higher FMI as compared to boys. In boys FMI showed a peak at 12+ years and declined thereafter while FMI continued to increase in girls up till 14+ years of age.

Comparison of median FMI also shows that FMI of girls was higher as compared to that of boys (Figure 4.3.7). Girls showed a sudden peak in FMI from 11+ years onwards owing to vigorous fat deposition in girls associated with puberty (Freedman et al, 2003).

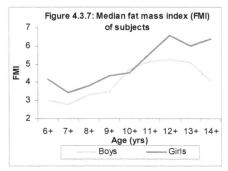

Figure 4.3.7: Median fat mass index (FMI) of subjects

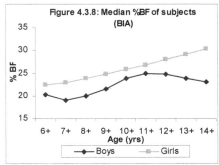

Figure 4.3.8: Median %BF of subjects (BIA)

4.3.3 Percent body fat (%BF)

As compared to FM, %BF is a more frequently cited measure in terms of the body composition literature. The means and standard deviations for %BF of boys and girls (n=1220) are given in Table 4.3.11. Details regarding percentiles of body fat are given in Appendix 8K.

Table 4.3.11: %BF of subjects

Ages (yr)	n	Boys Mean ± SD	n	Girls Mean ± SD	p-Value
6+	51	20.4 ± 7.2	47	23.9 ± 5.3	0.01
7+	64	18.4 ± 7.0	74	21.5 ± 6.3	0.01
8+	67	20.6 ± 6.1	62	23.1 ± 7.1	0.02
9+	108	21.4 ± 6.3	95	24.7 ± 6.8	0.001
10+	63	24.7 ± 7.9	53	25.9 ± 6.9	0.76
11+	85	25.1 ± 7.8	65	26.9 ± 6.6	0.14
12+	61	25.9 ± 7.9	46	28.8 ± 6.2	0.05
13+	107	23.8 ± 8.2	52	29.1 ± 6.7	0.01
14+	61	21.3 ± 9.6	59	30.2 ± 6.6	0.001

$p<0.05$ is statistically significant; Student's t-test

The mean %BF was significantly higher in girls as compared to boys at almost all age points. In boys values ranged between 18 and 25% body fat over the entire age range, with a peak at age 12+ years.

The comparison of median %BF between boys and girls is shown in Figure 4.3.8. There was a marked increase in positive skewness in body fat up to age 12+ years in boys. Both skewness and variability fell after age 12+ years. There was a steady increase in the median %BF of girls with increasing age and this increase continued till 14+ years. This is due to the fact that around puberty sex hormones induce a pronounced sexual dimorphism: boys gain proportionately more muscle and lean tissue compared to fat, and girls lay down fat as a natural part of the ontogeny of their sexual and reproductive physiology (McCarthy et al, 2006).

[A] Prevalence of adiposity

Although international interest in classifying health status according to adiposity is increasing, no accepted published ranges of %BF exist in children. The most widely used are the health-related %BF cutoffs of ≥25% body fat for boys and ≥30% for girls as proposed by Williams et al (1992).

Age wise percentage prevalence of adiposity in boys (%BF≥25%) and girls (%BF≥30%) is given in Table 4.3.12. Prevalence of adiposity among boys was higher during the pre-pubertal age group. Among girls, adiposity rates increased with increasing age. At age 6+ years, 31.4% of boys had body fat levels greater than 25% and 14.9% of girls had body fat levels greater than 30%. The overall adiposity rates were higher in boys (38.5%) as compared to girls (26.9%).

Table 4.3.12: Prevalence of adiposity using Williams et al cutoffs of ≥25% for boys and ≥30% in girls

Ages (yr)	Boys		Girls		p-Value
	n		n		
6+	51	16 (31.4)	47	7 (14.9)	0.01
7+	64	12 (18.8)	74	7 (9.5)	0.01
8+	67	18 (26.9)	62	10 (16.1)	0.02
9+	108	33 (30.6)	95	23 (24.2)	0.001
10+	63	28 (44.4)	53	12 (22.6)	0.76
11+	85	46 (54.1)	65	23 (35.4)	0.14
12+	61	34 (55.7)	46	20 (43.5)	0.05
13+	107	47 (43.9)	52	18 (34.6)	0.01
14+	61	23 (37.7)	59	29 (49.2)	0.001

Figures in parenthesis denote percentages
$p<0.05$ is statistically significant; Student's t-test

[B] Comparison with NHES I fatfold data

%BF estimated on the present study subjects from fatfolds using Slaughter et al (1988) equation were compared with %BF percentiles from NHES I fatfold data, also derived using the fatfold equations from Slaughter et al (1988) as recently given by Lohman and Going (2006).

Figures 4.3.9 and 4.3.10 depict that %BF was much higher in both boys and girls in the present study as compared to their US counterparts. In present study boys, the median lies in between the 85th and 95th percentile of NHES I while in girls the median is very close to the 95th percentile of NHES.

These data suggest that right from childhood, both boys and girls have a greater adiposity for a given BMI. It would therefore appear that the propensity of Indians to have higher adiposity begins right from childhood.

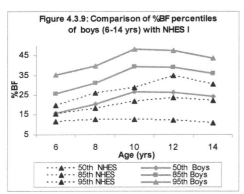
Figure 4.3.9: Comparison of %BF percentiles of boys (6-14 yrs) with NHES I

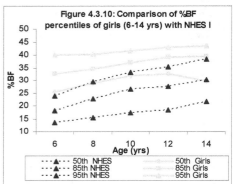
Figure 4.3.10: Comparison of %BF percentiles of girls (6-14 yrs) with NHES I

[C]   Comparison with NHANES III BIA data

The %BF and FFM computed from BIA of boys and girls in the present study, using Houtkooper's equation, was compared with the %BF and FFM values from the National Health and Nutrition Examination Survey (NHANES III) for 12-14 year old non Hispanic black males and females, non Hispanic white males and females and Mexican American males and females (Figures 4.3.11- 4.3.14).

In both boys and girls, %BF was the highest as compared to other ethnic groups; FFM was the lowest in these subjects.

Thus, data on FM computed from fatfold thicknesses or BIA, clearly demonstrate that Indian children have higher %BF as compared to other races.

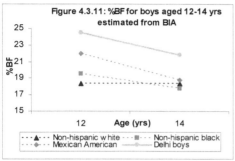

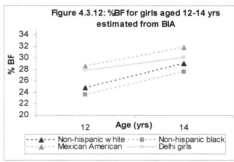

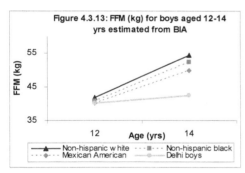

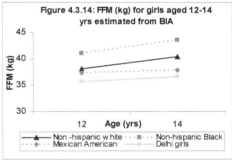

To sum up the findings on FMI and %BF of present study subjects:

- Median FMI of girls was higher as compared to that of boys. Girls showed a sudden peak in FMI from 11+ years onwards owing to vigorous fat deposition in girls associated with puberty.
- The %BF was significantly higher in girls as compared to boys at all age points.
- The overall adiposity rates as assessed by %BF cutoffs proposed by Williams et al (1992) were higher in boys (38.5%) as compared to girls (26.9%).

- Percent body fat computed from fatfold thickness data of present study subjects using Slaughter's equation were compared with. Percent body fat was much higher in both boys and girls in the present study as compared to the corresponding data from NHES I.
- %BF was the highest as compared to other ethnic groups; FFM was the lowest in these subjects.

4.3.4 Distribution of body fat

Several studies have shown that in adults the location of adipose tissue in addition to total body fat content is associated with metabolic disturbances. A male pattern of abdominal or central fat distribution is more detrimental to health than the female pattern of gluteal-femoral fat distribution in adults (Weststrate et al, 1989). Lately, it has been established that most disturbances related to abdominal obesity have their onset during childhood (Moreno et al, 2001). In children, body fat distribution may be described by a variety of procedures like imaging methods, CT MRI and DEXA, but the simplest ones are fatfolds and circumferences.

In the following section also, distribution of body fat is dealt selectively under two heads- fatfolds and circumferences.

[A] Fatfolds

Several fatfolds ratios have been also used to assess subcutaneous adipose tissue distribution (Moreno et al, 2001; Ketal et al, 2007).

In the present study, the ratios of triceps to subscapular and peripheral to truncal (biceps+triceps/ subscapular+suprailiac) as well as trunk to total fatfolds percent [(subscapular+suprailiac/biceps+triceps+subscapular+suprailiac)*100] were used as indices of subcutaneous body fat distribution in boys and girls. The triceps:subscapular and peripheral:truncal give the same information as trunk to total fatfolds percent i.e relative magnitude of truncal vs upper arm fatold thickness.

Figure 4.3.15 shows that both triceps:subscapular and peripheral:truncal decreased with increase in age up till 12+ years indicating a central subcutaneous fat distribution during pre-pubertal years in boys. Around the age of 13 years, there was an increase in both the ratios indicating redistribution of fat towards extremities before the onset of puberty in boys. For the same ages, a reverse trend was observed when trunk to total fatfolds percent was plotted again indicating a central subcutaneous fat distribution during the prepubertal years. As boys entered puberty around 13+ years, trunk to total fatfolds percent declined.

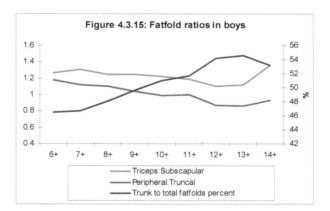

Among girls, a central subcutaneous fat distribution indicated by the decrease in both triceps:subscapular and peripheral:truncal, was observed up to the pubertal years (Figure 4.3.16). There was an increase in both the ratios around 13+ years indicating redistribution of fat towards extremities. The trunk to total fatfolds percent increased from 6+ years up to 12+ years and sharply declined thereafter.

Thus, redistribution of fat occurs around puberty; a more peripheral distribution in boys and a central distribution in girls.

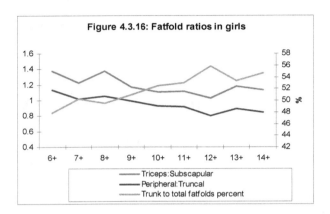

[B] Waist Circumference

Waist circumference in children has been shown to be an independent predictor of insulin resistance, lipid levels and blood pressure - all components of metabolic syndrome (Hirschler et al, 2005; Bacha et al, 2006; Lee et al, 2006, Flodmark et al, 1994). The recent International Diabetes Federation (IDF) definition of the metabolic syndrome in children includes waist circumference as mandatory criterion along with two or more other risk variables (Misra and Khurana 2008, Zimmet et al, 2007). Based on evidence from several studies (Bloch et al, 1987; Maffeis et al, 2001; Ford et al, 2005), the IDF (2007) workshop has recommended the use the 90th percentile of waist circumference for defining abdominal obesity. Hence in the present study, prevalence of obesity was estimated using the 90th percentile of age and sex specific waist circumference developed for the present study subjects (Annexure 8E).

Age wise percentage prevalence of obesity (≥ 90th percentile of waist circumference) in boys and girls is given in Table 4.3.13. In girls, the prevalence of abdominal obesity was marginally higher at 10+ years and remained high during the pubertal years, thereafter declined. In boys, abdominal obesity rates were high right from 6+ years up to 12+ years and declined thereafter. Abdominal obesity was highest at 11+ years which was also the time of peak height and weight gain in boys. This is because redistribution of fat occurs during pubertal years. The overall prevalence of abdominal obesity was higher in boys (11.5%) as compared to girls (10.1%).

Table 4.3.13: Age wise prevalence of obesity using 90th percentile of waist circumference for boys and girls

Age (yrs)	Boys		Girls	
	n	≥ 90th percentile	n	≥ 90th percentile
6+	209	22 (10.5)	162	19 (11.7)
7+	199	25 (12.6)	189	18 (9.5)
8+	212	28 (13.2)	179	17 (9.5)
9+	205	19 (9.3)	190	12 (6.3)
10+	201	26 (12.9)	148	22 (14.9)
11+	202	27 (13.4)	190	21 (11.1)
12+	203	24 (11.8)	137	17 (12.4)
13+	231	20 (8.7)	130	9 (6.9)
14+	201	23 (11.4)	138	13 (9.4)
Total	**1863**	**214 (11.5)**	**1463**	**148 (10.1)**

Figures in parentheses denote percentages

Estimates of the prevalence of overweight and obesity in population groups are usually based on body mass index (BMI) (Bellizzi and Dietz, 1999; Cole et al, 2000), but it gives no indication about fat distribution. Waist circumference is particularly important as it is a good measure of abdominal obesity. It is easy to measure, reproducible and requires inexpensive simple equipment. In view of the observed relationships between waist circumference, intra-abdominal fat deposition and cardiovascular disease risk factors in children (Flodmark et al, 1994), waist circumference should be adopted as an additional measurement to BMI in children.

To sum up the findings on distribution of body fat among subjects in the present study:

- Redistribution of fat occurs around puberty; a more peripheral distribution in boys and a central distribution in girls.
- Prevalence of obesity based on waist circumference was higher in boys (11.5%) as compared to girls (10.1%).
- Fatfolds and waist circumference are cost effective, non-invasive, non-time consuming and widely applicable techniques, especially for large cohort studies. Waist circumference, particularly, is easy to measure and should be routinely measured along with other anthropometric measurements like BMI in children.

4.3.5 Relationship between BMI and %BF

Excess body fat is the hallmark of obesity. Because of the lack of simple, accurate methods for assessing body fat directly, anthropometric indices such as BMI are used as surrogates for body composition. Interpretation of results is difficult as BMI does not distinguish between weight associated with muscle mass from weight due to excess body fat (adiposity), hence two persons with the same amounts of body fat can have quite different BMI values. The relationship between BMI and total body fat differs in different populations and Indians have a higher body fat and higher abdominal adiposity for a given BMI as compared to Caucasians and African Americans (Deurenberg et al, 1998; Chandalia et al, 1999; Yajnik et al, 2003). Since obesity and increased fat deposition begin in early childhood (Rolland-Cachera et al, 1987; Eriksson et al, 2003; Kaur et al, 2005), there is a need to define the relation between BMI and %BF in children and adolescents.

In the present study, the relationship between %BF as assessed using BIA method, and BMI was studied with the goal of defining BMI cutoffs with the greatest sensitivity and specificity for detecting obesity among 6-14 year old affluent children.

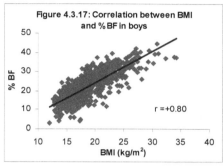

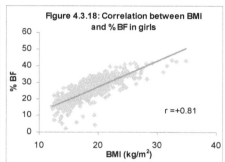

The %BF calculated by BIA method correlated strongly with BMI in both boys and girls (r= +0.80 for boys and +0.81 for girls, p<0.05) (Figures 4.3.17 and 4.3.18).

However, correlational analysis cannot describe the nature and extent of misclassifications, and when the purpose is to discriminate obesity from non-obesity, it is inappropriate to make recommendations based on correlations alone. Hence receiver operating characteristic curve (ROC) analysis was done to evaluate the performance of BMI in screening children and adolescents for excess body fat.

[A] ROC ANALYSIS

In the present study, excess fatness was defined using two %BF-based cutoffs, namely the ones proposed by Williams et al (1992) and Lohman and Going (2006). The results of Williams et al (1992) suggested a criterion of ≥25% body fat for boys and ≥30% for girls. These cutoffs were derived from body density as estimated from fatfold thickness measurements and exist only for overweight (or excess fatness).

Based on the results of Williams et al (1992), Lohman and Going (2006) suggested the healthy range of body fatness to be 10-25% for boys and 17-32% for girls. They recommended percent fat values greater than 30% for boys and 35% for girls to be used as cutoffs for screening obesity in children.

At different ages and stages of maturation, differences in body composition exist between males and females. Changes in body composition especially alterations in relative proportions of muscle and fat, are the hallmarks of pubertal maturation and result in typical male-female differences. For the same reason subjects were divided into two categories based on age, 6-9 years (prepubertal) and 10-14 (postpubertal) years.

The cutoffs of BMI corresponding to the criterion value with the best trade off (maximizing the sum of sensitivity and specificity) for 6-9 years and 10-14 year old boys and girls are presented in Tables 4.3.14 and 4.3.15. The Tables 4.3.14 and 4.3.15 also indicate the true positive (sensitivity) and false positive (1-specificity) rates corresponding to the cutoff values. For both sexes, the cutoffs for BMI increased predictably with age given the typical changes that occur in body weight and composition across the ages studied. The proportion of positives correctly identified (sensitivity) was greater than the proportion of negatives correctly identified (1-specificity) by BMI.

Table 4.3.14: Cut off value for BMI on ROC for overweight in boys and girls

Age group	Cut off	True positive rate (%)	False positive rate (%)	AUC (95% CI)
Boys				
6-9 yr (n=290)	17.7	94.9	17.6	0.95 (0.92-0.97)
10-14 yr (n=377)	19.4	90.4	23.0	0.91 (0.88-0.94)
Girls				
6-9 yr (n=280)	18.7	93.6	15.0	0.95 (0.92-0.97)
10-14 yr (n=273)	20.3	84.2	22.0	0.89 (0.85-0.93)

AUC: Area under the curve, CI: Confidence interval
The cutoff value corresponds to the best tradeoff between true positive and false positive rates to screen for overweight (≥25% body fat in boys and ≥30% body fat in girls; Williams et al, 1992)

Table 4.3.15: Cut off value for BMI on ROC for obesity in boys and girls

Age group	Cut off	True positive rate (%)	False positive rate (%)	AUC (95% CI)
Boys				
6-9 yr (n=290)	18.6	95.7	23.7	0.92 (0.88-0.96)
10-14 yr (n=377)	21.6	84.5	19.2	0.89 (0.86-0.93)
Girls				
6-9 yr (n=280)	20.1	100	13.9	0.95 (0.91-0.99)
10-14 yr (n=273)	22.1	94.1	18.2	0.94 (0.91-0.97)

AUC: Area under the curve, CI: Confidence interval
The cutoff value corresponds to the best tradeoff between true positive and false positive rates to screen for obesity (>30% body fat in boys and >35% body fat in girls; Lohman and Going, 2006)

Tables 4.3.14 and 4.3.15 also show the AUC estimates for BMI for the two age groups in boys and girls. All values were close to 1.0, suggesting good diagnostic accuracy of BMI as a tool for screening obesity in children and adolescents. The ROC curves along with the AUC for BMI of boys and girls in the two age categories are given in Annexure.

Studies by Lazarus et al (1996), Sardinha et al (1999) and Rao et al (2008) also used ROC curves to assess the usefulness of BMI for obesity screening in children and adolescents. Although there were methodological differences, the results of these studies were qualitatively similar to the present study and all supported the use of BMI as an obesity index in children and adolescents (Table 4.3.16).

Table 4.3.16: Studies showing true positive rate (sensitivity) and false positive rate (1-specificity) of BMI as an indicator of overweight/obesity as assessed by body fat

Author	Age group	True positive rate (%)	False positive rate (%)
Lazarus et al*	4-20 (B& G)	71.0	5.0
Sardinha et al*	10-11 (B)	96.0	14.0
	12-13 (B)	86.0	24.0
Rao et al**	9-16 (B)	74.2	34.9
	9-16 (G)	75.3	25.4
Present study**	10-14 (B)	90.4	23.0
	10-14 (G)	84.2	22.0

B: Boys, G: Girls; * body fat measured using DEXA; **body fat measured using BIA

Comparison of ROC cutoff of BMI with conventional BMI cutoffs: The ROC cutoffs obtained in the present study were compared with BMI-for-age z-scores given by WHO, 2007 and age and sex specific BMI cutoffs given by Cole et al, 2000. Table 4.3.17 clearly shows that the ROC cutoffs obtained for BMI in the present study were much lower compared to the conventional cutoffs emphasizing the fact that Indian children are more adipose at a lower BMI.

Table 4.3.17: Comparison of different BMI cutoffs

	ROC cutoff for Overweight*	ROC cutoff for Obesity**	WHO 2007^	Cole et al, 2000	
				$BMI \geq 25 kg/m^2$	$BMI \geq 30 kg/m^2$
6-9 yr					
Boys	17.7	18.6	20.1	18.8	22.2
Girls	18.7	20.1	21.0	18.7	22.2
10-14 yr					
Boys	19.4	21.6	24.2	21.6	26.4
Girls	20.3	22.1	25.6	22.1	27.2

Values for WHO 2007 and Cole 2000 BMI correspond to a mean age group of 8.5 years for boys and girls in the 6-9 yr category and to a mean age of 12.5 yrs in the 10-14 yr age category.
*using Williams et al (1992) cutoffs for boys and girls; **using Lohman and Going (2006) cutoffs for boys and girls
^Cutoff value for WHO 2007 corresponds to (+2)SD value

In a similar study on 9-16 year old affluent children in Pune, Rao et al (2008) also showed that ROC cutoffs for BMI improved sensitivity considerably, but the values were much lower compared to conventional cutoffs. They gave a cutoff of 19.7 kg/m^2 for 9-16 year old boys and 21.2 kg/m^2 for girls. These cutoffs agree with the present study viewing that the age range in the present study is little narrower. This was probably the only Indian study for predictions but done in Pune and not Delhi.

These observations suggest that BMI could be a reasonably good indicator, but may need a lower cutoff for assessing adiposity among affluent children and adolescents in Delhi.

[B] ROC analysis of other anthropometric variables

ROC analysis was also done to assess the usefulness of triceps and subscapular fatfolds, MUAC and waist circumference for screening children and adolescents with excess body fat. Excess body fat was defined as ≥25% body fat for boys and ≥30% for girls as suggested by Williams et al (1992).

The cutoffs of triceps, subscapular, MUAC and waist circumference corresponding to the criterion value with the best trade off (maximizing the sum of sensitivity and specificity) are presented in Table 4.3.18 for boys and Table 4.3.19 for girls in the two age groups. The true positive (sensitivity) and false positive (1-specificity) rates corresponding to the cutoff values are also given.

For both sexes, the cutoffs for triceps, subscapular, MUAC and waist circumference increased with age. The triceps and subscapular fatfold thickness cutoffs increased more in girls than in boys, whereas MUAC and waist circumference cutoffs increased more in boys than girls. These changes are consistent with the greater gains in muscle and bone experienced by boys during adolescence and greater gains in total body fat and subcutaneous adipose tissue experienced by girls (Sardinha et al, 1999).

Table 4.3.18: Cut off value for triceps, subscapular, mid upper arm and waist circumferences to screen for overweight in boys (≥25% body fat in boys; Williams et al, 1992)

BOYS	Triceps (mm)	Subscapular (mm)	MUAC (cm)	WC (cm)
6-9 yr (n=290)				
Cutoff	13.6	8.8	21.4	61.1
True positive rate (%)	84.8	88.6	87.3	87.3
False positive rate (%)	4.8	15.2	16.7	15.7
10-14 yr (n=377)				
Cutoff	14.0	12.4	24.5	71.4
True positive rate (%)	93.2	85.9	75.1	75.1
False positive rate (%)	20.0	13	21.5	9.5

Table 4.3.19: Cut off value for triceps, subscapular, mid upper arm and waist circumferences to screen for overweight in girls (≥30% body fat in girls; Williams et al, 1992)

GIRLS	Triceps (mm)	Subscapular (mm)	MUAC (cm)	WC (cm)
6-9 yr (n=280)				
Cutoff	14.6	11.6	21.5	62.2
True positive rate (%)	91.5	91.5	93.6	87.2
False positive rate (%)	15.9	22.7	20.6	14.2
10-14 yr (n=273)				
Cutoff	16.2	15.4	23.7	67.5
True positive rate (%)	85.2	87.1	82.2	76.2
False positive rate (%)	23.7	24.3	20.8	12.1

Table 4.3.20: Areas under the ROC curves for boys and girls in the two age categories

Group	Triceps (mm)	Subscapular (mm)	MUAC (cm)	WC (cm)
Boys				
6-9 yr (n=290)	0.95 (0.93-0.98)	0.94 (0.91-0.97)	0.92 (0.89-0.95)	0.93 (0.90-0.96)
10-14 yr (n=377)	0.93 (0.90-0.95)	0.92 (0.90-0.95)	0.84 (0.80-0.88)	0.89 (0.86-0.93)
Girls				
6-9 yr (n=280)	0.95 (0.92-0.97)	0.91 (0.87-0.95)	0.93 (0.89-0.96)	0.93 (0.89-0.96)
10-14 yr (n=273)	0.87 (0.83-0.91)	0.87 (0.83-0.91)	0.88 (0.83-0.92)	0.87 (0.86-0.93)
95 % CI in parenthesis				

Table 4.3.20 gives the AUC estimates for triceps and subscapular fatfold thicknesses, MUAC and waist circumference for the two age categories of boys and girls. Among 6-9 yr old boys and girls, the AUCs for triceps and subscapular fatfolds, MUAC and waist circumference were not significantly different from each other and were also close to the AUC of BMI (0.95; Table 4.3.14). All values were close to 1.0, suggesting good diagnostic accuracy of all these anthropometric variables as tools for screening obesity in the 6-9 year age group. In boys aged 10-14 years, AUCs of triceps and subscapular were not significantly different and were even higher than the AUC of BMI (0.91, Table 4.3.14). In the 10-14 years old girls, AUCs for triceps and subscapular fatfolds, MUAC and waist circumference were similar.

Overall, the results suggest that triceps and subscapular fatfold thicknesses and MUAC and waist circumferences were reasonable alternatives to BMI for assessing adiposity among affluent children and adolescents in Delhi.

[C] Prevalence of obesity using various indicators

The accurate identification of the obese child in health screening programmes for early intervention is of paramount importance. Several indicators and various standards have been proposed to assess obesity in children and adolescents. As a result reported studies show a large variation in the criteria used for the assessment of obesity among children and adolescents (Dietz, 1999). There is considerable disparity in the estimates of obese children obtained by different indicators.

Currently a variety of indicators like weight-for-age, BMI-for-age, %BF, fatfold at triceps and waist circumference are being used for assessing obesity. Prevalence of obesity was assessed by these indicators: weight-for-age (CDC, 2000), BMI-for-age (WHO, 2007) and adiposity as assessed by %BF (based on cutoffs proposed by Williams et al, 1992), triceps fat fold (Lohman and Going,

2006) and waist circumference (≥ 90th percentile, IDF, 2007). The data is shown in Figures 4.3.19 and 4.3.20 for present study boys and girls respectively.

There was considerable disparity in the estimates of obese children obtained by different indicators. Clearly BMI-for-age was a better indicator for detection of over-nutrition as compared to weight-for-age (22.8% vs.12.0% in boys; 12.9% vs. 8.5% in girls) (Figures 4.3.19 and 4.3.20). BMI-for-age is useful in identifying short and overweight children with high BMI and in identifying tall and lean children with lower BMI. A recent global survey on child growth monitoring practices (de Onis et al, 2004) showed that weight-for-age was the anthropometric indicator universally used (97% of countries), while only 23% of the countries used weight-for-height, with BMI being rarely used.

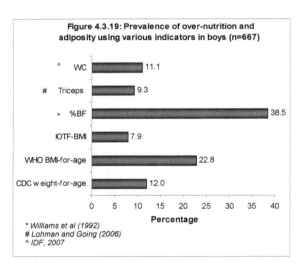

The prevalence rate of over-nutrition was lowest when IOTF-BMI cutoff values (Cole et al, 2000) corresponding to BMI of 30 kg/m^2 at age 18 were used, about one third the estimated rates using WHO 2007 in boys and about half the estimated rates in girls (Figures 4.3.19 and 4.3.20).

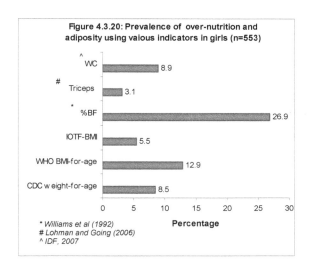

Figure 4.3.20: Prevalence of over-nutrition and adiposity using vaious indicators in girls (n=553)

* Williams et al (1992)
# Lohman and Going (2006)
^ IDF, 2007

The WHO 2007 reference is based on the distribution of representative samples of the US population. In contrast, the IOTF reference considers BMI cut-off points that are unrelated to the true distribution of the reference populations. In fact, child cutoff points are those which are extrapolated from a BMI of 25 and 30 at age 18; it is assumed that children with those BMI present inherent health risk. The difference in the origin of those cut-off points may explain in part why the absolute prevalence of obesity is different. A number of reports have shown that the IOTF-BMI cutoffs substantially underestimate the prevalence of childhood obesity in different populations (Kain et al, 2002; Fu et al, 2003; Wang and Wang, 2002).

However, BMI-for-age compared to %BF as an indicator, identified a much lower percentage of over-nourished subjects (Figures 4.3.19 and 4.3.20). In other words, adiposity rates were substantially high in boys (38.5% vs. 22.8%) and almost double in girls (26.9% vs. 12.9%) when %BF was used as indicator as compared to WHO 2007 BMI-for-age; this is attributable to the fact that Indian children have higher body fat for any BMI as compared to Caucasian children. It is possible that the differences in %BF may be even higher if the right equations validated by DEXA are available and used for computation of body fat in Indian children. In view of the importance of body fat as a determinant of risk of diabetes and cardiovascular disease in adult life, it is essential that high priority is given to validation of equation for computation of body fat using anthropometric measurements and BIA in Indian children using DEXA (three or four compartment model) or other appropriate techniques for accurate assessment of body composition.

As compared to adiposity rates using triceps, adiposity rates were higher if waist circumference was used as the indicator (11.1% vs. 9.3% in boys; 8.9% vs. 3.1% in girls) suggesting that the children had truncal adiposity (Figures 4.3.19 and 4.3.20). Also, peripheral adiposity (triceps fatfolds) rates were marginally less than the overall adiposity rates (9.3% vs. 38.5% in boys; 3.1% vs. 26.9% in girls) suggesting that truncal adiposity might to be responsible for a higher percent fat among the subjects. The high adiposity rates using waist circumference as an indicator over triceps fatfolds further strengthens this point. Hence among Indian children, truncal measurements could be a better predictor.

Since it is the excess body fat rather than excess body weight that is detrimental to health, the use of the BMI alone to evaluate overweight and obese individuals may lead to undesirable misclassifications. Hence obesity should ideally be defined on the basis of body fat.

Metabolically obese, normal weight individuals, not deemed obese on the basis of height and weight parameters, were found to be hyperinsulinaemic, hypertriglyceridaemic, insulin-resistant and predisposed to type 2 diabetes mellitus (Tanaka et al, 2002; Ruderman et al, 1998). The subjects in the present study belonged to well-to-do families of professionals, high officials and businessmen who had access to latest technologies and everyday conveniences making them more sedentary, which may predispose them to increased adiposity. Thus, there is a need to supplement BMI with other diagnostic criteria, in particular, ones that focus on body adiposity, considered both alone and with regard to its distribution.

Thus prevalence of obesity was also estimated using the ROC cutoffs obtained for BMI, triceps and subscapular fatfolds, MUAC and waist circumference (Table 4.3.21; Figures 4.3.21 and 4.3.22). The purpose was to investigate the relative performance of different indicators for screening children and adolescents with excess body fat.

Boys

In 6-9 year old boys, the overall prevalence of obesity was highest based on BMI cutoffs. In other words, BMI identified maximum number of boys with body fat ≥ 25%. Subscapular fatfolds, MUAC and waist circumference also gave close estimates to BMI. However, triceps identified the lowest number of boys with excess body fat (Figure 4.3.21).

Among 10-14 year old boys, BMI and triceps performed equally well as indicators of adiposity. Subscapular, MUAC and waist circumference gave lower estimates; least being for waist circumference (Figure 4.3.21).

Table 4.3.21: Prevalence of overweight using derived ROC cutoffs (≥25%BF for boys; ≥30% BF in girls)				
Indicator	Boys		Girls	
	6-9 yrs (n=290)	10-14 yrs (n=377)	6-9 yrs (n=280)	10-14 yrs (n=273)
BMI (kg/m^2)	111 (38.4)	206 (54.8)	79 (28.3)	123 (44.9)
Triceps (mm)	77 (26.6)	205 (54.5)	80 (28.7)	127 (46.4)
Subscapular (mm)	102 (35.3)	179 (47.6)	96 (34.4)	130 (47.5)
MUAC (cm)	104 (36.0)	176 (46.7)	92 (33.0)	119 (43.4)
Waist circumference (cm)	102 (35.3)	152 (40.3)	74 (26.5)	98 (35.8)
Figures in parenthesis dente percentages				

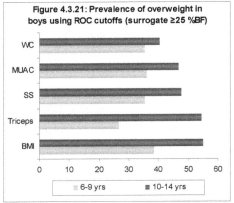

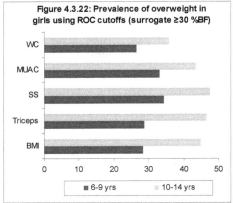

Figure 4.3.21: Prevalence of overweight in boys using ROC cutoffs (surrogate ≥25 %BF)

Figure 4.3.22: Prevalence of overweight in girls using ROC cutoffs (surrogate ≥30 %BF)

Girls

In 6-9 year old girls, the overall prevalence of obesity was highest based on cutoffs derived for subscapular fatfolds followed by MUAC while in the 10-14 year old age group, both fatfolds i.e subscapular and triceps may be used as indicators of adiposity (Figure 4.3.22).

Hence in boys 6-14 yrs, BMI represents a robust screening tool that can be used easily in field studies to screen school boys with excess body fat. Triceps can be used as an indicator of adiposity for 10-14 year old boys and girls. Subscapular fatfolds can be used for 6-14 year old girls. However, waist circumference underestimated as compared to other indicators.

Viewing height and weight as ubiquitous techniques the overweight/obese screening based on BMI is most useful. Other indicators support this conclusion.

To sum up the findings on relationship between BMI and %BF:

- There was a good correlation between %BF and BMI in both boys (r=+0.80) and girls (r=+0.81).

- Based on the ROC analysis, equivalent BMI cutoff corresponding to a body fat of ≥25% (adiposity) was 17.7 kg/m^2 and 19.4 kg/m^2 for 6-9 years and 10-14 years old boys respectively. For girls, the BMI cutoff corresponding to a body fat of ≥30% (adiposity) was 18.7 kg/m^2 for 6-9 years and 20.3 kg/m^2 for 10-14 years.
- ROC cutoffs obtained for BMI were much lower compared to the conventional cutoffs based on WHO 2007 and Cole et al, 2000 in both boys and girls.
- Triceps and subscapular fatfolds and MUAC and waist circumferences also proved to be good screening tools and hence reasonable alternatives to BMI for assessing adiposity among affluent children and adolescents in Delhi.
- The prevalence of over-nutrition as assessed by BMI-for-age was higher as compared to weight-for-age (22.8% vs.12.0% in boys; 12.9% vs. 8.5% in girls)
- Over-nutrition rates were lower, about one third the estimated rates using WHO 2007 in boys and about half the estimated rates in girls when the IOTF-BMI cutoffs.
- Adiposity rates were substantially high in boys (38.5% vs. 22.8%) and almost double in girls (26.9% vs. 12.9%) when %BF was used as indicator as compared to WHO 2007 BMI-for-age
- Adiposity was more truncal (higher proportion above the cut off for waist circumference as compared to those above the cut off values for triceps fatfold).
- The prevalence of obesity estimated using the ROC derived cutoffs showed that in boys 6-14 yrs, BMI represents a robust screening tool that can be used easily in field studies to screen school boys with excess body fat. Triceps can be used as an indicator of adiposity for 10-14 year old boys and girls. Subscapular fatfolds can be used for 6-14 year old girls. However, waist circumference underestimated as compared to other indicators.

4.4 PHYSICAL ACTIVITY PATTERN AND FOOD HABITS

Two major factors that affect the energy status in school children are physical activity and food intake (Yao et al, 2003). Even among the public school children 3.0% of boys and 1.3% of girls had low BMI-for-age while 16.2% of boys and 9.3% of girls had high BMI-for-age using CDC 2000 (Tables 4.2.32 and 4.2.33).

The purpose was to study the physical activity pattern and food habits in the two extremes of the continuum i.e. over-nourished and under-nourished. Hence information on activity pattern was collected on 81 subjects (boys and girls) between 8-10 years of age. These children were placed in two groups on the basis of their BMI: Group O (>+2SD of the BMI-for-age, CDC 2000; n=47) and Group U (<-2SD of the BMI-for-age, CDC 2000; n=34). Food habits of these children were also studied.

4.4.1 Physical activity

Physical activity is a behaviour involving movement of the body through space. Humans perform obligatory and discretionary physical activities (FAO/WHO/UNU, 2004).

Obligatory activities can seldom be avoided within a given setting, and they are imposed on the individual by economic, cultural or societal demands (e.g. daily activities such as going to school, tending to the home and family and other demands made on children and adults by their economic, social and cultural environment).

Discretionary activities, although not socially or economically essential, are important for health, well-being and a good quality of life in general. These are activities undertaken in the individual's discretionary free time and is selected on the basis of personal needs and interests. It includes household chores, socially desirable activities and activities aimed at maintenance of physical fitness.

[A] Leisure time physical activity

The various activities performed by the subjects after school during their leisure hours are shown in Table 4.4.1. The most preferred leisure time activities have been described in detail.

Table 4.4.1: Types of activities performed during leisure hours by 8-10 year old subjects (N=81)

Leisure time activities*	Overweight n=47	Underweight n=34
Lying/ resting	19 (40.4)	9 (26.5)
Leisure reading	23 (48.9)	14 (41.2)
Doing homework/ academic reading	47 (100.0)	34 (100.0)
Playing indoor with toys/ younger siblings/ games (e.g. hide and seek)	8 (17.0)	5 (14.7)
Chatting with friends/ relatives	23 (48.9)	15 (44.1)
Watching TV/ movie	43 (91.5)	32 (94.1)
Music lesson/ playing instrument	5 (10.6)	3 (8.8)
Playing videogame/ surfing internet	27 (57.4)	15 (44.1)
Painting	3 (6.4)	1 (2.9)
Exercise (yoga/ walking/ jogging)	2 (4.3)	0
Dancing (western/ classical)	6 (12.8)	4 (11.8)
Sports (coaching classes for cricket/ football/ tennis/ badminton; kabaddi, skipping, cycling)	16 (34.0)	10 (29.4)

Figures in parenthesis denotes percentages
*Numbers in categories overlap hence will not add up to the total number.

TV: Subjects reported preference for indoor activities like television viewing and other small screen activities (like electronic games and computers). TV viewing emerged as the most favorite past time among majority of subjects in both the groups. Subjects reported watching TV mostly during lunch hours i.e. immediately after reaching home from school and while having dinner than during any other time of the day. Subjects in Group O were spending up to 2.0 ± 0.76 hours daily on television viewing after school and this was significantly more than the time spent by Group U (1.5 ± 0.67) (Table 4.4.2).

Upto 57.4% of subjects in Group O and 44.1% of subjects in Group U had access to computers or videogames at home. In urban areas, lack of appropriate play area and limited open space around home along with heavy traffic make it difficult for children to play outdoors and as a result they are forced to engage in indoor games or watch television (Laxmaiah et al, 2007, Bhardwaj et al, 2008).

Table 4.4.2: Mean time spent on TV viewing, doing homework and in sports and exercise (hr/d)			
	Group O (n=47)	Group U (n=34)	p-Value
After school hours of television viewing	2.0 ± 0.8	1.5 ± 0.7	0.03*
Doing homework/academic reading	1.9 ± 0.6	2.2 ± 0.7	0.10
Sports and exercise	1.3 ± 0.6	1.4 ± 0.7	0.52
$p<0.05$ is statistically significant; Student's t-test			

Homework: High burden of school work, emphasis on tuitions and academic competitiveness have also led to decreased participation in sports and other forms of physical activity. The time spent on homework by 6-9 year olds in United States increased from 44 minutes per week in 1981 to more than 2 hours in 1997; the corresponding estimates for 9-11 year olds were 2 hours and 49 minutes in 1981 and more than 3.5 hours per week in 1997 (Malina and Katzmarzyk, 2006).

Table 4.4.2 shows the time spent doing academic work by the subjects in the two groups. Leisure reading i.e. story books, novels, newspaper reading were not included in this category. Eight to ten year old subjects in the present study spent upto 2 hours daily doing homework or studying at home/tuitions (Group O: 1.9 ± 0.6 hr/d; Group U: 2.2 ± 0.7 hr/d; p=NS). The subjects in the two groups did not differ significantly in the time spent doing homework (Table 4.4.2).

Sports: Table 4.4.1 also shows data on participation in various organized activities like extra curricular activities (art, music, dance or sports). The classes were usually held twice or thrice a week. Among the instruments played were casio, guitar and piano. Dancing was reported by 10 subjects and all were girls.

Sports were enjoyed by 34.0% of Group O subjects and 29.4% of Group U subjects both in school and at home. Cricket and football were the popular sports. Among the others were badminton and tennis. Extra classes for cricket and football were held in schools also and subjects used to reach early to school for practice. Apart from sports played after school, compulsory physical training classes were held in school once a week. In school going children, physical activity is related to school curriculum, especially during the ages 8-15 years (Kurpad et al 2004). Gavarry et al (2003) showed that school days increased the habitual physical activity of children compared to school free days in their study of 182 children between the ages of 6-20 years. Further compulsory activity at school made a difference for children. In contrast to the observations on school going children and adolescents, in primary school children aged 7 to 10.5 years, the total amount of physical activity did not depend on the duration of physical education timetabled at school, as these children compensated by being active out of school (Mallam et al, 2003).

The exercise pattern of subjects shows that only two subjects belonging to Group O exercised and rest did not. Both these subjects spent 30-40 minutes doing yoga combined with moderate intensity walking and had been doing so regularly for over 20 days. Easwaran et al (2001) reported that exercise should be done for a minimum of 30 minutes, if done for lesser duration all the benefits of exercise are not there.

Table 4.4.2 shows the mean time spent on sports and exercise out of the school hours (physical training classes in school and sports played during lunch break have not been included). The time spent on sports and exercise did not differ significantly in Group O (1.3 ± 0.6 hr/d) and Group U (1.4 ± 0.7 hr/d) subjects; these subjects were physically active for more than over an hour during their discretionary free time.

[B] Mode of transport to school

All subjects reported using vehicular transport such as school bus (n=23, 48.7% in Group O; n=14, 41.2% in Group U) or cars (n=24, 51.1% in Group O; n=20, 58.8% in Group U) to reach school (Figure 4.4.1). None of the subjects in either group walked to school highlighting the fact that physically active transport to work (or school) has declined while the potential for physical inactivity has increased tremendously.

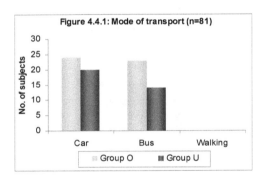

[C] Time spent on various habitual activities

The actual time (hours/day) spent on various habitual activities by the two groups was also studied. The habitual activities were grouped into 3 broad domains, consisting of sedentary activities (all sedentary activities at school and home), moderate to rigorous activities (physical training at school, games and exercise at and after school) and sleep and the data is given in Table 4.4.3

Time spent sleeping was not statistically different in the two groups while time spent performing sedentary activities and watching television were significantly higher (p<0.05) in Group O as compared to Group U. The time spent in moderate to rigorous activities was not different among Group O and Group U subjects.

Table 4.4.3: Time spent on select habitual activities (hr/d)				
Group	MET range (Kcal/min)	Group O	Group U	p-Value
Sleep	1.0	8.8 ± 1.1	9.1 ± 0.8	0.18
Sedentary	Less than 3.0	8.0 ± 1.1	7.4 ± 0.9	0.02*
Moderate to rigorous	3.0-8.0	1.6 ± 1.0	1.4 ± 0.6	0.34
TV viewing/ computer/ videogames	1.6	2.0 ± 0.8	1.5 ± 0.7	0.03*

Reported values are mean ± SD; hr/d: hours per day; does not total to 24 hrs
*Significant at p<0.05; Student's t-test

In the present study, obese children were more sedentary and spent more time in sedentary pursuits like television viewing. Maffeis et al (1996) also reported that 8-10 year old obese children from Italy, spend less time in physical activity, more time in sedentary activities and rest. The time spent on moderate and rigorous activities were not different among normal and obese subjects in their study also. The American Academy of Pediatrics (2001) recommended that the children's total media time (TV, video and video games) to be limited to no more than 1 to 2 hours per day.

[D] TDEE

The energy expenditure of the subjects belonging to Group O and Group U was assessed for one working day. The calculated BMR, TDEE, $EE_{(sleep)}$, $EE_{(rigorous\ activities)}$ and $EE_{(sedentary\ activities)}$ are tabulated and given in Table 4.4.4.

The mean BMR and TDEE along with its components i.e. $EE_{(sleep)}$, $EE_{(rigorous\ activities)}$ and $EE_{(sedentary\ activities)}$ were significantly higher in Group O as compared to Group U. PAL i.e the ratio between TDEE / BMR were not significantly different in the two groups (1.6 ± 0.22 in Group O and 1.5 ± 0.19 in Group U).

BMR, which represents the largest portion of daily energy expenditure (50-75%) (Fukagawa et al, 1990) is calculated using equations that are weight dependent; higher the weight of the subject, higher is the BMR. Low BMR and TDEE in group U was primarily due to weight dependent calculations, hence time spent on various activities delineate some of the differences in the BMI status of these subjects.

Table 4.4.4: BMR and energy expenditure of Group O (n=47) and Group U (n=34) subjects

Group	Weight (kg)	BMI (kg/m^2)	BMR (Kcal/d)	TDEE (Kcal)	EE$_{(sleep)}$ (Kcal)	EE$_{(sedentary)}$ (Kcal)**	EE$_{(rigorous)}$ (Kcal) **	PAL
Group O	46.1 ± 7.9	24.3 ± 2.5	1505 ± 202.5	2378 ± 486.5	533 ± 91.2	630 ± 239	547 ± 404	1.6 ± 0.2
Group U	27.5 ± 5.6	14.1 ± 2.3	1121 ± 175.1	1636 ± 175	402 ± 63	447 ± 92	300 ± 124	1.5 ± 0.2
p- Value	0.001	0.001	0.001	0.001	0.001	0.001	0.006	0.090

Reported values are mean ± SD; p<0.05 is statistically significant
Used Student's t-test; ** Used Two-sample Wilcoxon rank-sum (Mann-Whitney) test

The trends seem to suggest an increase in the number of sedentary behaviours among these subjects: watching television, playing videogames, personal computer activities, homework, extra curricular classes (tutoring, art, music), motorized transport to school and other organized activities.

Thus it is suggested that it could be critical to have preadolescent children maximize their exposure to various activities at a young age to enhance the likelihood that they will maintain participation in some of these activities in later years (Kurpad et al, 2004)

4.4.2 Food habits

[A] Diet pattern

Majority of the subjects were non-vegetarians (n=32; 68.0% in Group O and n=22; 65.0% in Group U), about 30.0% vegetarians (n=14 in Group O and n=11 in Group U) and 2-3% ovo-vegetarians (n=1 in both Group O and Group U) (Figures 4.4.2 and 4.4.3). Among the non vegetarians, chicken was preferred by followed by mutton (n=25; 46.3%) and fish (n=10; 18.5%). The data revealed overall inclination towards non-vegetarianism in both the groups. With weekends as off days for most working parents, they mostly consumed non-vegetarian food on weekends. Nutritionally, non-vegetarian foods enhance the quality of protein intake.

[B] Meal pattern

Meal pattern followed by most of the subjects irrespective of their BMI status was consistent on a weekday as well as on weekends and is given in Table 4.4.5. Meal pattern of the subjects varied from as low as three meals to as high as six meals on a working day. The only subject from Group O who reported consuming three meals a day was doing so for religious purposes. Most subjects consumed five meals on weekdays (n=37, 78.7% in Group O; n=31, 91.2% in Group U) and weekends (n=44, 93.6% in Group O; n=31, 91.2% in Group U). The five-meal pattern comprised breakfast, lunch and dinner with midmorning snack (tiffin) and evening tea.

[C] Meal skipping pattern

The meal skipping pattern of subjects was studied and the results are depicted in Table 4.4.6. There was no difference in the meal skipping pattern between the two groups.

Of the total eighty one subjects studied, majority (n=66) followed a regular meal pattern and did not skip any meals. Breakfast was consumed regularly by these subjects before leaving for school. All reported having milk everyday in the morning along with fruit/ biscuits/ egg/ upma/ cornflakes. These 8-10 year old subjects spent more time eating at home than they did in school. Their food choices and food preferences were thus largely dependent on what their parents and caregivers provided.

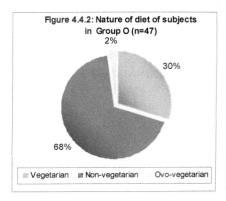

Figure 4.4.2: Nature of diet of subjects in Group O (n=47)

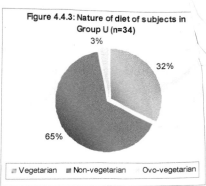

Figure 4.4.3: Nature of diet of subjects in Group U (n=34)

Table 4.4.5: Number of meals consumed by subjects

No. of meals	Group O (n=47)		Group U (n=34)	
	Weekday	Weekend	Weekday	Weekend
2	0	0	0	0
3	1 (2.1)	0	0	0
4	4 (8.5)	0	3	1 (2.9)
5	37 (78.7)	44 (93.6)	31 (91.2)	31 (91.2)
6	5 (10.6)	3 (6.4)	0	2 (5.9)

Figures in parenthesis denotes percentages

Table 4.4.6: Meal skipping pattern of subjects

	Category	Group O (n=47)	Group U (n=34)
Meal skipping	Yes	7 (14.9)	8 (23.5)
	No	40 (85.1)	26 (76.5)
		Group O (n=7)	Group U (n=8)
Frequency of skipping meals	Daily	0	1 (12.5)
	Alternate days	0	0
	Once a week	2 (28.6)	2 (25)
	Occasionally	5 (71.4)	5 (62.5)
*Frequency of missing particular meals	Breakfast	6	5
	Mid-morning snack (tiffin)	5	4
	Lunch	1	1
	Evening tea/snack	4	4
	Dinner	2	2

Figures in parenthesis denotes percentages
*Numbers in categories overlap hence will not add up to the total number

Almost similar number of subjects in Group O and Group U reported skipping meals. Of the fifteen subjects who reported skipping meals, majority (n=10) of subjects skipped meals only occasionally. Only one subject from Group O reported skipping his midmorning snack daily stating lack of hunger as the reason. Majority (n=6 in Group O and n=5 in Group U) reported missing breakfast followed by mid-morning snack (n=5 and n=4 in Group O and Group U respectively).

The reasons for skipping breakfast were listed as getting late for school, waking up late, not feeling hungry and busy doing homework. The school timings were from 7:45 a.m. to 1:15 p.m. Children coming from far off places had to leave homes as early as 6:45 a.m. making them time pressed in the morning leading to skipping breakfast and visiting the canteen during midmorning. Upto 93.8% (n=76) frequently visited the canteen. Post dinner eating prevented two subjects from consuming breakfast. Breakfast usually follows a fast of 10-12 hours. Studies have shown that nutrients which are missed at breakfast are not generally compensated for later in the day (Morgan et al, 1986).

Subjects who missed their midmorning snack, reported lack of hunger as the major deterrent. Some of the other reasons cited were dislike for what they got from home or practicing for some extra curricular activity during the recess time.

Only two children reported missing lunch and the reasons stated were lack of hunger due to canteen use (chips/ kurkure/ spring rolls/ lime soda) as a part of friend's birthday treat or dislike for what was cooked at home.

Evening snack was missed by 8 subjects, the reasons being rushing for tuitions or heavy lunch. Only four subjects reported missing dinner, three stated lack of hunger due to evening partying out as the reason and one did not give any specific reason.

[D] Canteen use

The frequency of canteen use and the foods preferred by subjects are given in Table 4.4.5. The trends were similar in the two groups. About 5 subjects (6.2%) did not use the canteen at all. Among the rest (n=76, 93.8%) canteen use was common. Of these 76 subjects (93.8%) who visited the canteen, 3 subjects (n=2 from Group O and n=1 from Group U) visited canteen every alternate day mainly for chips or a beverage. Majority (n=40, 88.9% from Group O; n=27, 87.1% from Group U) reported canteen use only once in a week, mostly on fridays. This one day was fixed by parents and their kids were allowed to carry money to school and buy whatever they liked either from the canteen or the hawkers outside. Most subjects carried their tiffins on this day also.

Table 4.4.7: Canteen use by subjects			
	Category	Group O (n=47)	Group U (n=34)
Canteen use (n=81)	Yes	45 (95.7)	31 (91.2)
	No	2 (4.3)	3 (8.8)
Frequency		Group O (n=45)	Group U (n=31)
	Daily	0	0
	Alternate days	2 (4.4)	1 (3.2)
	Once a week	40 (88.9)	27 (87.1)
	Occasionally	3 (6.7)	3 (9.7)
*Foods preferred (based on methods of cooking)	Baked (Sandwich/idli/pastries, pizza)	19 (42.2)	13 (41.9)
	Fried (Samosa/springroll/chowmein/vada)	45 (100.0)	28 (62.2)
	Pressure cooking (Rajma/chole chawal)	8 (17.8)	7 (22.6)
	Others (Bhelpuri/kurkure/chips/funflips)	42 (93.3)	28 (62.2)
*Beverages preferred (n=70)	Flavoured milk	2 (4.4)	1 (3.2)
	Tea/coffee	0	0
	Nimbu soda	40 (88.8)	28 (62.2)
**Desserts	Ice-cream	36 (80.0)	27 (87.1)

Figures in parenthesis denotes percentages
*Numbers in categories overlap hence will not add up to the total number. ** ice-cream was not sold in the canteen, available with hawkers

Most popularly selected items were fried foods like samosas, spring rolls followed by junk foods like chips and kurkure (Table 4.4.7). Nimbu soda was the most popular beverage among all students and its consumption was seen even in winter months of the study. Ice-creams were relished by most of the subjects and were available with the hawkers outside the school.

Carbonated drinks were not sold at all in the schools that were a part of the study. These schools were conscious of the fact that soft drinks offer energy with little accompanying nutrition, displace other nutrient sources, and are linked to several key health conditions such as diabetes and hence had banned the sale of soft drinks inside the school.

The data shows clearcut preference for fast foods and ice-creams over traditional foods like chole/rajma chawal or flavoured milk. Healthy eating patterns need to be fostered at this stage as it will form the basis of their dietary habits for the future. This was also visible when they chose to dine outside (Figure 4.4.4).

[E] Eating out pattern

The frequency of eating out as reported by subjects is shown in Table 4.4.8. It can be seen from the data gathered that frequency of eating out was not different among Group O and Group U subjects. For most subjects the frequency of eating out ranged from once on weekends (n=29, 31.9% in Group O and n=10, 29.4% in Group U) to once a month (n=15, 61.7% in Group O and n=22, 64.7% in Group U). About 6.2% (n=5) ate out every alternate day.

Subjects chose from a wide variety while eating out. Among the most preferred cuisines were Italian and Chinese followed by fast foods like burgers, french fries and soft drinks (Figure 4.4.4). As a result the most frequented eating joints were Pizza Hut, Yo China and Mc Donalds (Figure 4.4.5).

Table 4.4.8: Eating out pattern of subjects

	Category	Group O (n=47)	Group U (n=34)
Frequency of eating out	Daily	0	0
	Alternate days	3 (6.4)	2 (5.9)
	Once a week	29 (31.9)	10 (29.4)
	Occasionally	15 (61.7)	22 (64.7)

Figures in parenthesis denotes percentages

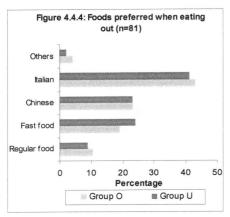

Figure 4.4.4: Foods preferred when eating out (n=81)

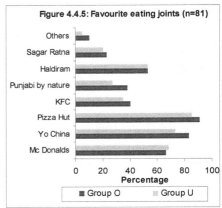

Figure 4.4.5: Favourite eating joints (n=81)

Globalization and free trade have brought fast-food eating establishments to most countries, especially to developing nations. Consumption of franchised fast foods, either for meals or a snack is becoming popular as evident from the increasing number of fast food restaurants (Lee et al, 1994). Fast food restaurant use was reported by 37% of adults and 42% of children in US (Paeratakul et al, 2003). Such a trend, shifting from home based eating habits to restaurant foods, also has an impact on the food habits of children.

Consumption of regular food i.e. food similar to the kind eaten at home was reported by 13.5% of subjects (n=8) only (Figure 4.4.6). Vijayapushpam et al (2003) reported that higher socioeconomic adolescents in India, preferred fast foods to traditional foods and irrespective of income group, most children consumed carbonated beverages.

Thus, early childhood is likely to be an important period for intervention as lifetime habits are established. These subjects will soon enter adolescence which is a period of immense change. It involves a transition from childhood dependency to adult self-sufficiency. When children are young, their parents and families have greater control over what they eat. As they get older, however, what their friends eat in the school environment, and what is available to them in school and elsewhere, will have an impact on what they eat. Nutrition education in food habits needs to be imparted at this stage to improve their dietary intakes. Children should be given assistance in selecting appropriate behaviors for their health needs, rather than being guided by their own (often inaccurate) perceptions of their weight.

Schools play an important role in encouraging healthy behaviours in children. The school curricula should include messages about diet, physical activity and television viewing, altering school environments to provide more healthy food and beverage options and promoting walking to school. Physical education must be compulsorily integrated into the school curriculum and emphasis should be placed on sports and activities rather than drills/ exercises as desired by subjects.

To sum up the findings on physical activity pattern and food habits of the subjects in the present study:

- TV viewing emerged as the most favorite leisure time activity among majority of subjects in Group O (n=43; 91.5%) and Group U (n=32; 94.1%).
- Eight to ten year old subjects in the present study spent upto 2 hours daily doing homework or studying at home/tuitions (Group O: 1.9±0.6 hr/d; Group U: 2.2±0.7 hr/d; p=NS).

- The time spent on sports and exercise did not differ significantly in Group O (1.3±0.6 hr/d) and Group U (1.4±0.7 hr/d) subjects; these subjects were physically active for more than over an hour during their discretionary free time.
- All subjects reported using vehicular transport such as school bus (n=23, 48.7% in Group O; n=14, 41.2% in Group U) or cars (n=24, 51.1% in Group O; n=20, 58.8% in Group U) to reach school (Figure 4.4.1). None of the subjects in either group walked to school.
- Time spent sleeping was not statistically different in the two groups. However, Group O spent more time performing sedentary activities (8.0 ± 1.1 vs. 7.4 ± 0.9; p<0.05) as well as watching TV (2.0 ± 0.8 vs. 1.5 ± 0.7) compared to Group U.
- The physical activity pattern of 81 subjects, 8-10 years old showed that TDEE was significantly higher in Group O as compared to Group U (2378 ± 486.5 vs. 1636 ± 175; p<0.05). $EE_{(sleep)}$, $EE_{(moderate\ to\ rigorous\ activities)}$ and $EE_{(sedentary\ activities)}$ were also significantly higher in Group O as compared to Group U.
- Majority of the subjects were non-vegetarians (n=32; 68.0% in Group O and n=22; 65.0% in Group U), about 30.0% vegetarians (n=14 in Group O and n=11 in Group U) and 2-3% ovo-vegetarians (n=1 in both Group O and Group U).
- A five meal pattern was followed on weekdays (n=37, 78.7% in Group O; n=31, 91.2% in Group U) and weekends (n=44, 93.6% in Group O; n=31, 91.2% in Group U).
- Of the total eighty one subjects studied, majority (n=66) followed a regular meal pattern and did not skip any meals.
- Canteen use was common (n=76, 93.8%) among both the groups.
- Most popularly selected items by both groups when eating out including school canteen were fast foods and fried snacks.

4.5 PUBLIC SCHOOL VS. GOVERNMENT SCHOOL BOYS

A total of 90 boys from a government school and 108 boys from public schools were studied. Comparison was made between 9 year old boys from the public schools and a government school in terms of their anthropometry and body fat. The means and standard deviations for all the anthropometric variables and body fat of public school and government school boys are given in Table 4.5.1.

Table 4.5.1: Physical characteristics of public school and government school boys

Variable	Public school boys (n=108)	Government school boys (n=90)	p-value
Weight (kg)	32.8 ± 7.0	23.8 ± 4.3	0.001
Height (cm)	136.5 ± 6.2	127.2 ± 7.1	0.023
BMI (kg/m^2)	17.5 ± 2.8	14.6 ± 1.6	0.001
MUAC (cm)	21.4 ± 3.4	17.0 ± 2.0	0.001
Triceps (mm)	11.7 ± 4.8	6.2 ± 2.6	0.005
Biceps (mm)	7.2 ± 2.9	4.4 ± 1.9	0.003
Subscapular (mm)	9.9 ± 5.0	5.7 ± 2.7	0.001
Suprailiac (mm)	9.9 ± 6.0	4.8 ± 3.4	0.001
Waist circumference	60.9 ± 7.8	54.4 ± 5.5	0.001
Hip circumference	71.2 ± 7.3	62.7 ± 5.2	0.010
%BF	21.4 ± 6.3	14.6 ± 4.3	0.001

Reported values are mean ± SD; p<0.05 is statistically significant
Student's t-test

As expected public school boys were significantly taller and heavier and had a higher BMI compared with their age matched counterparts from government school. All circumferential measurements, fatfold thickness and computed body fat measurements were significantly higher in public school boys as compared to government school boys (Table 4.5.1).

4.5.1 Prevalence of under-nutrition and over-nutrition (WHO 2007)

Prevalence of under and over-nutrition was assessed using three indices: weight-for-age, height-for-age and BMI-for-age according to WHO 2007 standards and is given in Table 4.5.2 and Figure 4.5.1.

Table 4.5.2: Prevalence of under- and over-nutrition in public and government school boys using WHO 2007

	n	< (-2) SD	(-2) to (+2) SD	> (+2) SD
Weight-for-age				
Public school	108	0	92 (85.2)	16 (14.8)
Government school	90	24 (26.6)	66 (73.4)	0
Height-for-age				
Public school	108	1 (0.9)	103 (95.4)	4 (3.7)
Government school	90	30 (33.3)	58 (64.4)	2 (2.2)
BMI-for-age				
Public school	108	4 (3.7)	82 (75.9)	22 (20.4)
Government school	90	11 (12.2)	77 (85.6)	2 (2.2)

Figures in parentheses denote percentages

Prevalence of stunting (<mean-2SD of height-for-age) and underweight (<mean-2SD of weight-for-age) was higher in government school boys. Stunting which is indicative of previous or long standing under-nutrition affected 33.3% of government school boys. Stunting (0.9%) was not seen among public school boys. Whereas 26.6% of government school boys were underweight (<mean-2SD of weight for age) using weight for age as the criteria, 14.8% were overweight (>mean+2SD of weight for age) among public school boys.

Percentage prevalence of over-nutrition (>mean+2SD of BMI for age) was higher using BMI-for-age, about 20% among HIG boys and 2.2% among the government school boys and under-nutrition (<mean-2SD of BMI for age) rates were 3.7% in public school boys as compared to 12.2% among government school boys. This is because, as compared to weight, BMI as an index is useful in identifying short and overweight children with high BMI and in identifying tall and lean children with lower BMI (Figure 4.5.1).

Thus, there are significant differences in anthropometric parameters of children belonging to public and government schools with public school children being significantly taller and heavier. In a recent study, Bhardwaj et al (2008) showed that prevalence of obesity among adolescent children was 29.0% in private schools and 11.3% in government funded schools. Similar trend has been reported by several other studies within the country (Marwaha et al, 2006, Ramachandran et al, 2002, Chatterjee, 2002).

This significant disparity in anthropometric parameters between the two socioeconomic strata from the same geographical area, with a high prevalence of overweight and obesity among public school subjects, is indicative of the problem of rampant dual nutrition burden.

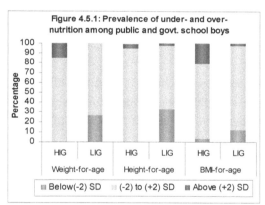

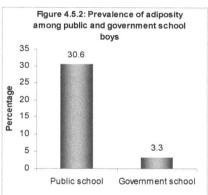

4.5.2 Prevalence of adiposity

In order to explore the level of adiposity, body fat was estimated using BIA in boys studying in government schools and compared with that of public school boys. Government school boys had a significantly lower %BF as compared to boys studying in public schools (Table 4.5.1). Using body fat cutoff of ≥ 25% for obesity in boys based on the work of Williams et al (1992), adiposity was determined in the two groups and is given in Figure 4.5.2. Prevalence of over-nutrition was higher among subjects if %BF was used as indicator as compared to weight for age and BMI for age; this is attributable to the fact that Indian children have higher body fat for any BMI as compared to Caucasian children. Adiposity rates were ten times higher among public school boys (n=33, 30.6%) as compared to government school boys (3.3%, n=3).

To sum up:

- Public school boys were significantly taller and heavier and had a higher BMI compared to age matched boys from government school.
- All the three circumferential measurements, four fat fold thicknesses and computed %BF were also significantly higher in public school boys as compared to government school boys signifying higher adiposity levels.
- Stunting affected 33.3% of government school boys. Stunting (0.9%) was not seen among public school boys.
- About 26.6% of government school boys were underweight (<median-2SD of weight-for-age) and none were overweight using weight-for-age as the criteria, 14.8% of public school boys were overweight (>median+2SD of weight-for-age).
- Percentage prevalence of over-nutrition (>median+2SD of BMI-for-age) and under-nutrition were higher using BMI-for-age as an indicator of nutritional status as compared to weight-for-age in both government and public school boys.
- Under-nutrition (<median-2SD of BMI-for-age) rates were 3.7% in public school boys as compared to 12.2% among government school boys. Over-nutrition (>median+2SD of BMI-for-age) was prevalent among 20% of public school boys and 2.2% among the government school boys.
- Prevalence of over-nutrition was higher among subjects if %BF was used as indicator as compared to weight-for-age and BMI-for-age.
- Adiposity rates were ten times higher among public school boys (30.6%) as compared to government school boys (3.3%).

CPSIA information can be obtained
at www.ICGtesting.com
Printed in the USA
LVHW041345140123
736914LV00008B/580